Mom's All Time Favourite Cookbook

by
Diana Norminton

ISBN 0-88925-709-4

Copyright © 1986

Photography by Jim Schibler
Cover features Special Pepper Steak, Page 38

Printed and Bound in Canada
by
Friesen Printers
16644-117 Ave.
Edmonton, Alberta
T5M 3W2

Contents

MEAT, FISH, EGG, CHEESE

Introduction

Every kitchen has its favourite recipes and favourite dishes which are frequently used because they are applauded by family and friends. My kitchen is no different. This high regard for my collection of recipes has prompted me to compile this cookbook.

Some of the recipes in this book date back to my grandmother's day. Many of them came to me on little slips of paper after having the pleasant experience of enjoying the dishes at family gatherings. Throughout the book, recipes which date back to my childhood days, as well as those that came my way more recently, have become favourites in my kitchen because they are practical, palatable, pleasing, and delicious! I am thrilled at the prospect of putting this collection into your kitchen for your enjoyment!

SPECIAL NOTES

Oven Temperature

When a recipe requires oven baking, the oven should always be preheated to the temperature stated in the recipe. All temperatures are given in Fahrenheit. An oven conversion table for your convenience is given below:

200 degrees F. = 100 degrees C.
275 degrees F. = 140 degrees C.
300 degrees F. = 150 degrees C.
325 degrees F. = 160 degrees C.
350 degrees F. = 180 degrees C.
375 degrees F. = 190 degrees C.
400 degrees F. = 200 degrees C.
425 degrees F. = 220 degrees C.
450 degrees F. = 230 degrees C.

When baking in pyrex or other ovenproof glassware, reduce the temperature by 25 degrees F. or 10 degrees C.

Measures

All measures are given in standard kitchen utensil form, i.e., cup, teaspoon, tablespoon, with the exception of ounces (oz.) in the "The Little Extras" section where liquid measure is required. One ounce of liquid is equivalent to 2 tablespoons or $1/8$ of a cup.

Ingredients

When using salt in a recipe, it is safer to under salt than to over salt the dish. In the recipes of this collection, where it is called for, salt has been used, but used quite sparingly. If you find a recipe needing more salt to suit your taste, do not hesitate to increase the amount to your liking.

Many of the recipes in this collection call for butter, however, margarine can be used as a substitute with no change to the flavour of the dish with the exception of some pastries. For example, in the case of shortbread, margarine can make the pastry dough more salty than is desired. Margarine is not as perishable as butter, but I prefer dairy products to oils in my cookery.

Tips

Helpful hints, given as Mom's Helpers, are given in this collection of recipes to make kitchen chores less time consuming. The tips included in this book have been an invaluable help to me many a time in my busy schedule. You may find them as useful techniques in helping save time or simply interesting and informative.

MEAT,
FISH,
EGG,
and
CHEESE
DISHES

BEEF'N GREEN ONION QUICHE

5 eggs
1/2 lb. ground beef
1 cup cream
2 1/2 cups seasoned bread stuffing mix
1 tsp. Worcestershire sauce
1/2 tsp. salt
2 cups green onions, finely chopped
1 cup swiss cheese, shredded
3-4 drops tabasco sauce
Paprika

Preheat oven to 400 degrees F. In a large mixing bowl, beat 1 egg slightly. Add 1/2 cup cream and stuffing mix. Mix lightly and let stand for 5 minutes, then add beef, Worcestershire sauce, salt, and 1/4 cup green onions. Mix only until combined. Spoon lightly into bottom and sides of 9-inch pie plate and shape into crust. Sprinkle remaining green onions over beef crust. In separate bowl beat 4 eggs until foamy, (about 5 minutes by electric mixer), then stir in cheese, tabasco, and remaining 1/2 cup cream. Pour over onions onto meat crust. Sprinkle lightly with paprika and bake 35-40 minutes. When done, a knife inserted into the center should come out clean. Serves 6-8.

CHEDDAR BEER FONDUE

1/4 cup butter
1/4 cup flour
1/4 tsp. dry mustard
1 1/2 cups beer
1 tsp. Worcestershire sauce
3 cups shredded cheddar cheese
Bread cubes or bread sticks and/or raw vegetables

Melt butter in a medium saucespan, blend in flour and mustard. Gradually stir in beer and Worcestershire sauce. Cook over medium heat, stirring until smoothly thickened and mixture comes to a boil. Reduce heat to low, add cheese and stir until melted. Transfer to a fondue pot and keep warm over a burner. Serve with bread cubes or sticks or raw vegetables as dippings.

Mom's Helpers

When reheating quiche in a microwave oven, place on a napkin or paper towel prior to reheating to avoid a soggy crust.

CHEDDAR 'N' ONION QUICHE

    1   unbaked 9-inch pie shell
1$^1/_4$ cups finely chopped onion
    3   tbsp. butter
    2   cups shredded cheddar cheese
1$^1/_2$ tbsp. flour
 $^1/_2$ tsp. salt
    5   eggs
1$^1/_2$ cups light cream
       paprika

Bake pie shell in preheated 425 degree F. oven 5 to 7 minutes. Reduce heat to 325 degrees F. Saute onion in butter until tender. Cool. Add cheese, flour and salt. Toss lightly to combine. In a separate bowl beat eggs well. Stir in cream. Add cheese mixture and pour into partially baked shell; sprinkle lightly with paprika. Bake at 325 degrees F. for 40 to 45 minutes. Serve hot. Makes 6 servings.

CHEESE FONDUE WITH WINE

2$^1/_2$ tbsp. butter
2$^1/_2$ tbsp. flour
    1   clove crushed garlic
1$^1/_2$ cups milk
    1   cup finely shredded swiss cheese
    4   well beaten eggs
 $^1/_2$ cup dry white wine
       Salt and pepper

In a fondue pot or heavy saucepan, melt butter over medium heat. Stir in flour and garlic. Cook for 2 minutes. Add milk, stirring constantly, until mixture is smooth and begins to thicken. Reduce heat to low, add cheese. Stir until smooth. Beat eggs and wine together and add to sauce. Season to taste. Cook over low heat until mixture just begins to set, but is soft. Serve with chunks of crusty brown bread, croissants, or toasted bread cubes.

Mom's Helpers

Hard-cooked egg yolks will not discolor if you chill eggs immediately after cooking.

To bake a souffle that is evenly cooked throughout, place the dish in a shallow pan of hot water while the souffle bakes.

CHEESE SOUFFLE

3 tbsp. butter
1 cup milk
$^1/_8$ tsp. pepper
$^1/_4$ tsp. Worcestershire sauce
1 cup grated milk white cheese
$^1/_3$ cup flour
$^1/_2$ tsp. salt
$^1/_4$ tsp. dry mustard
4 eggs, separated
1 tbsp. red wine

Melt butter in a saucepan. Add flour all at once and stir until blended. Gradually pour in milk. Stir sauce over low heat 3-4 minutes. Remove from heat and add salt, pepper, dry mustard and Worcestershire sauce. Beat egg yolks and add a little of the hot sauce to egg yolks. Mix well and gradually add remaining sauce. Cook over low heat for 1 minute, stirring constantly. Remove from heat and add cheese and wine. Stir well and cool completely. Beat egg whites until stiff. Fold in cheese sauce into egg whites until well blended. Turn into 1$^1/_2$ quart souffle dish and bake at 350 degrees F. for 45 minutes, or until knife inserted into center comes out clean. Serves 4-6.

CHEEZY POTATO PUFF

1$^1/_2$ cups grated cheddar cheese
$^1/_4$ cup butter
3 cups hot mashed potatoes
3 beaten egg yolks
$^2/_3$ cup milk
1$^1/_2$ tsp. salt
$^1/_8$ tsp. pepper
$^1/_4$ tsp. dry mustard
3 egg whites

Combine cheese and butter with potatoes. Combine remaining ingredients except egg whites and add to potato-cheese mixture, beating until smooth. Beat egg whites until stiff peaks form, then fold into potato mixture. Turn into greased baking dish. Bake at 350 degrees F. for 40 to 45 minutes. 6 to 8 servings.

Mom's Helpers

For quiches, partially bake pie shell for 10 minutes. Remove from oven and set aside. Reduce oven temperature to 350 degrees F. when baking the pie, unless otherwise stated.

CRAB MEAT QUICHE

  3 tbsp. butter
  3 tbsp. green onions
  4 eggs
1¹/₂ cups crab meat (or shrimp)
  2 tbsp. dry white vermouth or dry white wine
  1 cup 32 per cent cream (whipping cream)
  1 tbsp. tomato paste
 ¹/₂ cup cheddar cheese, grated
    Salt and pepper to taste
  1 9-inch pie shell

Bake pie shell for 8 minutes at 450 degrees F. Cool. Beat eggs and cream, add tomato paste, salt and pepper. Add crab meat and vermouth to onions. Simmer for a minute to allow wine to evaporate. Combine fish mixture with eggs and cream mixture. Pour into pie shell, sprinkle with cheddar cheese. Bake 30-35 minutes. Serves 4-6.

CRUNCHY CHEESE BALL

  1 pkg. 8 oz. softened cream cheese
 ¹/₄ cup mayonnaise
  2 cups ground cooked ham
  2 tbsp. chopped parsley
  1 tsp. minced onion
 ¹/₄ tsp. dry mustard
 ¹/₄ tsp. hot pepper sauce
 ¹/₂ cup chopped peanuts or walnuts

Beat cream cheese and mayonnaise until smooth. Stir in next 5 ingredients. Cover; chill several hours. Form into balls; roll in nuts to coat. Serve with assorted crackers.

Mom's Helpers

Before adding sour cream to a sauce that must boil, stir a teaspoon of flour into the cream. You can let the sauce boil and bubble safely. The flour prevents the sour cream from curdling.

A large egg contains 80 calories — 60 in the yolk, 20 in the white. The white is an excellent source of protein for a weight loss diet.

CRUSTLESS QUICHE

1 tbsp. butter or margarine
4 eggs
1 cup sliced onions
3/4 tsp. salt
2 cups evaporated milk
1/8 tsp. cayenne pepper
3/4 cup swiss cheese, grated
1/2 cup fine bread crumbs

In medium skillet, melt butter or margarine. Saute onions, stirring occasionally, until limp but not brown. Spread in buttered 9-inch pie plate. Beat together eggs, evaporated milk, bread crumbs, salt and cayenne until just blended. Pour over onions. Sprinkle cheese on top. Bake for 30-40 minutes, or until center is set and top is golden in color, at 350 degrees F. Serves 4.
For variety, replace the onion with cooked bacon, chopped ham, or sliced mushrooms.

DIETER'S QUICHE

4 eggs
1/2 cup cooked ham, diced
1 1/2 cups cooked beef, diced
2 tbsp. green pepper, chopped
1 tbsp. chives, chopped
8 oz. creamed cottage cheese
1/2 tsp. dry mustard
Dash pepper

Lightly beat the eggs in a medium sized bowl. Stir in ham, cottage cheese, green pepper, chives, and mustard. Add pepper. Spoon into greased small casserole dish or 4 individual baking dishes. Bake in 350 degree F. oven for about 40 minutes or until a knife inserted into the center comes out clean. Serves 4. Calories: 280 per serving. (Cottage cheese can be creamed very easily if put into a food processor for 30 seconds before using it in the recipe).

Mom's Helpers

A few drops of lemon when washing lettuce will keep it crisp and remove any insects and soil.

To prevent eggs shells from cracking while eggs are being boiled, sprinkle a teaspoon of vinegar over them in the water. Works beautifully.

Open-Face Tuna Broil, Page 17

INDIVIDUAL QUICHES

Pastry for 2-crust pie
$^3/_4$ cup chopped cooked shrimp
$^1/_4$ cup chopped green onion
4 oz. swiss cheese, shredded
$^1/_2$ cup mayonnaise
2 eggs
$^1/_3$ cup milk
$^1/_4$ tsp. salt
$^1/_4$ tsp. dried dill weed

On floured suface roll half of pastry dough into 12-inch circle. Cut six 4-inch circles. Repeat with remaining pastry. Fit into twelve $2^1/_2$ inch muffin pan cups. Fill each with some shrimp, onion, and cheese. Beat remaining ingredients. Pour over cheese. Bake in 400 degree F. oven 15 to 20 minutes or until browned. Makes 12. These are creamy and very easy to hold.

MACARONI AND CHEESE CASSEROLE

$1^1/_2$ cups cooked macaroni
10-12 slices bacon
$^1/_2$ cup finely chopped onion
4 tbsp. butter
4 tbsp. flour
1 tsp. salt
$1^3/_4$ cups milk
2 cups shredded cheddar cheese
1 cup dairy sour cream

Drain macaroni. Broil bacon, turning to cook both sides; drain; set aside. In a medium saucepan saute onion in butter until tender. Blend in flour and salt. Gradually stir in milk. Cook over medium heat, stirring constantly until smoothly thickened and mixture comes to a boil. Reduce heat to low. Add cheese and sour cream. Stir until cheese is melted. Combine sauce and macaroni. Pour into a greased 2-quart casserole. Arrange cooked bacon on top. Bake in preheated 350 degrees F. oven 25 to 30 minutes. Serves 5.

Mom's Helpers

Grate a quantity of cheese; spread on baking sheet and freeze. Store in plastic bags or containers and use as needed for casserole dishes, toppings, and omelets.

Always fold heavy mixture into beaten egg whites rather than whites into the mixture, as less air is forced out of whites in this process.

MUSHROOM QUICHE

- 1¹/₂ cups sliced mushrooms (canned)
- ³/₄ cup swiss cheese, grated
- 4 eggs
- 2 tbsp. green onion, finely chopped
- 1 cup cream
- ¹/₄ tsp. salt
- Dash of pepper
- ¹/₈ tsp. tarragon flakes
- Pastry for two 9-inch pie crusts

Line pie plates with pastry and bake 8 minutes at 450 degrees F. Cool. Spread mushrooms, grated cheese, and green onion over bottom of pie shells. Combine eggs, cream and seasonings, and beat well. Pour into pie shells. Bake at 400 degrees F. for 25 to 30 minutes, until center is solid.

QUICHE LORRAINE

- 6-8 slices bacon
- 3-4 green onions, finely chopped
- 1¹/₂ cups swiss cheese, grated
- 3 eggs
- 1³/₄ cups light cream (10 percent)
- 1 tbsp. flour
- ¹/₂ tsp. salt
- ¹/₈ tsp. nutmeg
- few grains cayenne pepper
- 1 9-inch pie shell

Partially bake pie shell for 10 minutes at 400 degrees. F. Remove from oven and set aside. Drop oven temperature to 350 degrees F. Chop bacon and cook until crisp; drain well. Sprinkle bacon, onions, and grated cheese into pie shell. Beat eggs until yolks and whites are blended, then mix in cream, flour, salt, nutmeg and cayenne. Pour into pie shell. Bake at 350 degrees F. for 35-40 minutes or until center is set when a test knife is inserted.

Mom's Helpers

To keep sauteed mushrooms light in color, cook them in butter over moderate heat. Add a few drops of lemon juice and water. Do not use a black iron skillet.

To keep the mixing bowl still while you stir or beat in it, place the bowl on a wet, folded kitchen towel.

TUNA QUICHE

1-7 oz. tin chunk white tuna
1 tbsp. butter
$^1/_2$ cup green chopped onion
$^1/_3$ cup swiss cheese, grated
4 eggs
1$^1/_2$ cups cream
2 tbsp. chopped parsley
$^1/_2$ tsp. salt
Paprika
Dash pepper and nutmeg
1 9-inch pie shell

Bake pie shell at 450 degrees F. for 8 minutes. Cool. Saute onion about 2 minutes in butter. Beat eggs then add in onion, cream, parsley, salt, pepper, nutmeg, tuna, and cheese. Pour into partially baked shell. Sprinkle with paprika. Bake 35-40 minutes or until set at 350 degrees F. Let stand for about 10 minutes before serving. Serves 4-6.

Mom's Helpers

To cook asparagus easily, peel with a vegetable peeler, then tie them in a bunch and stand them upright in the bottom of a double boiler. Add 1$^1/_2$ inches of water and cover them with the inverted top of the double boiler.

For perfect poached eggs, add a drop of lemon to the cooking water.

Baked potatoes will not explode if you make a slit in the skin of the potato before putting it into the oven. This acts as an escape valve against the build-up of steam that can cause the explosion of a potato.

Eggs taken out of the refrigerator lose one day's freshness per hour.

BOSTON CLAM CHOWDER

    1 ten-oz. (approx.) can clams
    1 stalk diced celery
    2 small diced onions
 1/4 lb. diced salt pork
    2 medium diced potatoes
    1 cup water
    1 cup cream
       Parsley, salt and pepper to taste

Drain the clams and set them aside. Simmer the clam juice, celery and onions for 20 minutes, covered. Melt and brown the salt pork in a frying pan, add the potatoes and stir until they are well covered with fat. Drain off remaining fat. Add the clam juice mixture and the water to the potatoes and simmer for 20 minutes, or until the potatoes are cooked. Add the clams, cream, parsley, salt and pepper. Heat until very hot, but NOT boiling. Serves 4.

BROILED LOBSTER TAILS

    6 frozen lobster tails
       Seasoned salt
       Butter sauce

Twenty minutes before serving, place solidly frozen lobster tails, shell side up, on a cutting board. With a sharp knife, cut through the hard outer shell and meat of each, splitting tail in half but leaving end of tail intact. Bend each split lobster tail backwards so meaty inside is exposed and shell meets in the back. Place tails, shell side up, on broiler pan. Broil 5 minutes; turn with tongs, and broil 5 to 7 minutes or until flesh is opaque and tender.

CRAB GRAPE SALAD

    1 lb. cooked crab meat
 1 1/2 lbs. seedless grapes
    1 large avocado
    1 cup finely chopped celery
 1/2 cup mayonnaise mixed with 1/4 cup milk

Cut grapes in half and avocado in small pieces. Place in bowl with celery, seasonings and mix. Add salad dressing and toss lightly. Chill. Add crab meat just before serving and toss again lightly. Serve on lettuce leaves.

CREAMY SALMON CURRY

    1 cup salmon
    2 tbsp. butter
    2 tbsp. flour
    1 tsp. curry powder
 $^1/_2$ tsp. sugar
 $^1/_8$ tsp. ground ginger
    2 tbsp. minced onion
 $^1/_4$ tsp. salt
 $^1/_2$ cup salmon liquid (add milk to make up $^1/_2$ cup)
 $^1/_2$ cup light cream
 $^1/_2$ tsp. grated lemon rind
    2 cups cooked rice

Drain salmon, reserving liquid. Break salmon into bite size chunks. Heat butter; blend in flour, curry powder, sugar, ginger, minced onion, and salt. Slowly add mixed salmon liquid and milk, then add cream. Cook and stir over low heat until sauce is smooth and thickened. Do not allow sauce to boil. Add salmon and lemon rind; heat. Serve over hot cooked rice. Serves 4.

CRISPY CODFISH

    1 lb. fillet of fresh cod
    2 tbsp. soy sauce
    1 tbsp. chopped ginger
 $^1/_8$ tsp. salt
 $^1/_8$ tsp. pepper

Batter:

 $^2/_3$ cup cornstarch
 $^1/_3$ cup flour
    1 tsp. vinegar
 $^1/_2$-$^3/_4$ cup water
       cooking oil
    1 tbsp. baking powder

Cut cod into bite-size pieces and place into a bowl. Make a marinade of soy sauce, ginger, salt and pepper. Marinate chunks for 30 minutes, turning the pieces occasionally. Combine cornstarch, flour and vinegar. Add enough water to make a thick batter. Dip fish chunks into batter. Fry in hot oil until golden brown. Remove to a paper-towel covered plate and keep warm in oven until all fish is cooked. Serve with french fries. Serves 2-3.

CURRIED LOBSTER

1 tart, minced apple
1 minced onion
1 to 2 tbsp. lemon juice
1 tbsp. cornstarch
1 cup cream or chicken stock
1 tbsp. butter
1 to 2 tbsp. curry powder
1 lb. lobster

Mince apple and onion and sprinkle with lemon juice to prevent apple from turning brown. Combine cornstarch with cream or stock. Melt butter in frying pan. Add onion and apple and cook thoroughly. Sprinkle with curry powder, add cornstarch, creamed mixture, and lobster. Keep hot over low heat. Serve with boiled rice.

EASY CRAB BISQUE

6 oz. canned crab meat
1 pkg dried chicken noodle soup mix
2^1/$_2$ cups boiling water
2 cups undiluted evaporated milk
2 tbsp. sherry

Drain crab meat and break into bite-size chunks. Combine soup mix and water in large saucepan. Bring to boiling point, cover and simmer for 5 minutes. Slowly stir in evaporated milk. Add crab meat. Reheat to simmering temperature. Remove from heat and add sherry. Serves 6.

Mom's Helpers

If you cannot iron sprinkled clothes as soon as you had planned, put them in a plastic bag and place into the bottom of the refrigerator. They will keep for days without the risk of mildewing.

To check whether you have already salted your vegetables, dip a meat skewer into the water and then hold it over a flame. If it burns bright orange, the salt was added.

When freezing fresh water fish fillets, place them in clean plastic containers, fill with very cold water to fully cover and freeze immediately. When ready to use, thaw in the usual manner. This process helps retain the "freshly caught fish" flavour.

EXOTIC LOBSTER CURRY

    3 cups milk
    2 cups fresh or dried coconut
 $^{1}/_{2}$ cup butter
    5 onions, chopped
    2 minced garlic cloves
 $^{1}/_{8}$ tsp. cumin seed
    2 tsp. powdered ginger
       Dash of cayenne pepper
    2 tsp. salt
    2 tbsp. curry powder
    2 chopped tomatoes
    2 tbsp. flour
    1 cubed cucumber
       Meat from 2 boiled lobsters or 1 lb. lobster meat cubed
    2 tbsp. lemon juice
    1 tbsp. plum jam

Combine the milk and coconut in a saucepan. Bring to a boil and remove from the heat, and stand for 30 minutes. Press out all the milk from the coconut and discard the pulp. Melt the butter in a saucepan and add the onions and garlic. Saute for 10 minutes, stirring frequently. Add the cumin seed, ginger, cayenne pepper, salt, curry powder and tomatoes. Cover and cook over low heat for 10 minutes, stirring often. Add the flour and continue stirring. Add the coconut milk slowly, stirring steadily until the boiling point is reached. Add the cucumber and lobster meat and cook over low heat for 15 minutes. Mix the lemon juice and jam together and add to the lobster mixture. Adjust the seasoning if needed and mix well. Serve hot, with boiled rice. Additional curry may be added for those liking their dishes "hot".

FISH FILET

 $1^{1}/_{2}$ lbs. perch, halibut, cod or salmon
    1 tbsp. butter
    2 tbsp. finely chopped onions
    2 tbsp. parsley
 $^{1}/_{2}$ cup chopped stewed tomatoes
    3 tbsp. dry white wine
    1 cup water
 $1^{1}/_{2}$ tbsp. butter
 $1^{1}/_{2}$ tbsp. flour
    1 egg yolk

Place filets in buttered square pan. Cover with all ingredients except the $1^{1}/_{2}$ tbsp. butter, flour, and egg yolk. Bake in 375 degrees F. just until cooked. In small dish mix $1^{1}/_{2}$ tbsp. butter and flour into a paste. Pour off liquid from the baked filet into a small saucepan and blend in the paste. Stir in yolk and let boil for 2 minutes. Pour sauce over the filet, place back in the oven for 5 minutes. Serves 4.

FLAMING LOBSTER

   2 tbsp. olive oil
 $^1/_2$ cup chili sauce
 $^1/_2$ cup wine vinegar
   1 tsp. black pepper
   3 boiled lobsters, split in half
 $^1/_2$ cup rum heated

Heat the olive oil, chili sauce, vinegar, and pepper in a saucepan. Remove the lobster meat carefully and cut into large pieces, reserving the shells of the body. Add the lobster meat to the sauce and fill the shells with the mixture; pour heated rum over and set aflame just before serving.

HAWAIIAN LOBSTER WITH COCONUT

   2 cups milk
   2 cups light cream
   3 cups fresh or dried grated coconut
 $1^1/_2$ lb. lobster meat

Combine the milk, cream and coconut in a saucepan; bring to boil, remove from heat and allow to soak for 30 minutes. Press out all the liquid from the coconut and discard the pulp. Cut the lobster meat into 1 inch pieces and combine with coconut milk. Heat but do not boil. Serve hot or cold in bowls.

LEMON GLAZED FILLETS

   2 lbs. fish fillets (pike, trout, perch, pickerel or whitefish)
   1 tbsp. prepared mustard
   3 tbsp. lemon juice or juice or 1 lemon
 $^1/_2$ tsp. grated lemon rind
 $^1/_4$ cup brown sugar
   1 tsp. salt
      Thin lemon slices

Cut fillets into serving size pieces. Marinate fillets for half an hour in mixture of mustard, lemon juice, lemon rind, brown sugar and salt. Place fillets on greased broiler rack and place two to four inches from heating unit. Brown one side of fillets. Turn, baste and brown the other. During the last few minutes of cooking time, top with lemon slices. The glaze should bubble and brown. Allow 10 minutes cooking time for each one-inch thickness of fish. If fillets are browning too rapidly, lower the broiler rack. Serves 6.

LOBSTER MELT

2 lobsters, about 1¹/₂ lbs. each
²/₃ cup chopped mushrooms
3 tbsp. butter
3 tbsp. flour
¹/₄ tsp. salt
¹/₈ tsp. dry mustard
Dash of paprika
1¹/₂ cups milk
3 tbsp. sherry or lemon juice
3 tbsp. finely grated cheddar cheese

Prepare lobster, remove meat and save body shells. Cut the lobster into bite sizes. Melt 1 tbsp. of butter, add the mushrooms and pan fry until tender. Melt remaining butter in the top of a double boiler; stir in flour and seasonings. Add the milk slowly and cook over hot water, stirring constantly until thickened. Stir in the grated cheese and continue stirring until melted. Add the lobsters, mushrooms and sherry or lemon juice; mix well. When thoroughly heated, spoon into lobster shells arranged on a shallow baking dish. Sprinkle with finely grated cheese and broil 4 inches from the top heat for about 2 minutes or until cheese is a golden brown.

LOBSTER SALAD

2 cups cut up cooked lobster meat
1 cup thinly sliced celery
2 hard cooked eggs, coarsely chopped
Dash of salt and freshly ground pepper
1 tsp. lemon juice
2 tbsp. French dressing
¹/₂ cup mayonnaise
Lettuce
Lemon wedges

Combine lobster, celery, eggs and seasonings. Gradually add lemon juice and French dressing to mayonnaise. Combine with lobster mixture tossing lightly until well blended. Place on crisp lettuce cups and garnish with a wedge of lemon. (If desired, surround with slices of avocado which have been sprinkled with lemon juice to prevent darkening.)

Mom's Helpers

To remove fish and onion smells from your hands, dampen your hands and gently rub them with salt before washing them.

LOBSTER SOUFFLE

5 oz. lobster meat, canned
2 tbsp. butter
2 tbsp. flour
$^1/_2$ tsp. salt
1 cup milk
$^1/_2$ cup mayonnaise
3 egg whites
3 egg yolks

Drain and cut lobster into small pieces. Melt fat and blend with flour and salt; add milk gradually and cook and stir until sauce is thickened. Remove from heat. Stir in mayonnaise and beaten egg yolks. Add lobster in sauce. Fold beaten egg whites into slightly cooled sauce. Pour into ungreased 1$^1/_2$ quart casserole. Place in shallow pan of hot water and oven poach at 350 degrees F. for 45 minutes or until set and lightly browned.

LOBSTER SUPREME

6 boiled lobsters
$^1/_2$ cup butter
$^1/_2$ cup wine vinegar
2 tsp. sugar
1$^1/_2$ tsp. salt
$^1/_8$ tsp. pepper
$^1/_4$ tsp. nutmeg
Dash of cayenne pepper
1$^1/_2$ cup heavy cream
6 slices toast

Remove the lobster meat from the shell and cut into small cubes. Melt butter in saucepan; add lobster meat and cook over low heat for 5 minutes, stirring occasionally. Add the vinegar, sugar, salt, pepper, nutmeg and cayenne pepper; cook over low heat for 5 minutes but do not allow the mixture to boil. Remove from heat, add cream gradually, stirring constantly. Taste and adjust the seasoning if necessary. Place a slice of toast in each soup plate and pour some of the lobster mixture over it. Serves 6.

Mom's Helpers

When cooking fish, allow a half teaspoon of salt per pound, except for smoked or already salted fish. For boiling shrimp, use one teaspoon per one quart of water.

OPEN-FACE TUNA BROIL

1 cup flaked tuna
$^1/_3$ cup mayonnaise
$^1/_4$ cup commerical sour cream
2 tbsp. chopped parsley
2 tsp. lemon juice
$^1/_4$ tsp. garlic salt
4 buns, split in half
3 tbsp. butter
8 slices cheddar cheese

Combine the first 6 ingredients. Spread the butter on the bun halves. Place a heaping tablespoon of the tuna mixture on each bun. Place a slice of cheese over each mound. Place under broiler for 2 to 3 minutes, watching carefully to allow cheese to melt and lightly brown. Serve immediately.

SALMON APPETIZERS

1 can ($7^3/_4$ oz.) canned salmon
1 tbsp. mayonnaise
1 tbsp. sour cream
1 tsp. lemon juice
  Salt and pepper to taste
2 large cucumbers

Mash salmon with a fork, including juice and bones. Add mayonnaise, sour cream, lemon juice, and seasonings. Mix well. Cut off ends of cucumbers and peel. Scoop out seeds and centre with a long handled spoon, leaving a $^1/_2$ inch circular shell. Drain well and dry. Pack with salmon mixture. Chill. Cut in slices about $^1/_2$-inch thick. Serve on lettuce leaves. Garnish with olives. Serves 6.

SEASONED HALIBUT STEAK

4 halibut steaks
4 tsp. white wine vinegar
4 tbsp. blue cheese salad dressing
4 tsp. wheat germ
1 tsp. chopped chives

Sprinkle halibut steaks with vinegar and lay in shallow buttered baking pan. Spread top side of each steak with salad dressing. Sprinkle with wheat germ and then chives. Bake at 375 degrees F. for 25-30 minutes, or until fish flakes easily with a fork. Serves 4.

SPECIAL SHRIMP DISH

$^1/_3$ cup chopped sweet pickles
$^1/_2$ cup sweet pickle juice
$1^1/_4$ cups water
$^1/_3$ cup ketchup
   1 tbsp. soy sauce
      Salt and pepper to taste
   3 tbsp. cornstarch
   3 tbsp. cold water
   1 eight-ounce pkg. of frozen shrimp

Place pickles, juice, water, ketchup, and soy in a large saucepan and bring to a boil. Add salt and pepper to taste. Mix cornstarch with 3 tbsp. water to a smooth paste. Add to hot mixture, stirring constantly, until mixture boils and thickens — about 2 minutes. Cook shrimp by putting into boiling water. Simmer for 5 minutes. Drain and pour sauce over hot shrimp. Serves 4.

SPEEDY SALMON CHOWDER

   2 cups canned salmon
   2 cans (10 oz. each) condensed cream of potato soup
   3 cups salmon liquid (add milk to make the measure)
$^1/_2$ tsp. grated lemon rind

Drain salmon, reserving liquid. Break salmon into bite-size chunks. Crush soft bone with a fork and add it to the liquid. In a deep saucepan, combine soup with blended salmon liquid and milk. Heat gently, stirring often, until mixture begins to simmer. Add salmon and grated lemon rind. Reheat but do not let boil. (Boiling could curdle the liquid). Serves 6.

Mom's Helpers

To help small children determine the left shoe from the right, draw faces inside the shoes which must always look at each other.

To keep salt or pepper from going damp in the shaker, add a dried pea or a few grains of rice to absorb excess moisture.

STUFFED LOBSTER

6 lobsters, split
1 cup butter
2 chopped onions
1/4 lb. mushrooms, chopped
1 tbsp. flour
1/2 cup stock
1 tsp. salt
1/4 tsp. pepper
  Dash of cayenne pepper
1/2 cup bread crumbs
1/2 cup grated cheese

Remove the meat from the lobsters and cut in small pieces; reserve the shells. Melt 3 tbsp. butter in saucepan; add onions and mushrooms and saute for 15 minutes. Add flour, stirring constantly; add stock, continuing to stir until the mixture boils and cook for 15 minutes. Place the lobster mixture in the shell; sprinkle with bread crumbs and cheese; dot with remaining butter. Place on baking sheets and bake at 350 degrees F. for 15 minutes, or until lightly browned. Serve with lime or lemon wedges.

TARTAR SAUCE SPECIAL

3 tbsp. mayonnaise
1 tbsp. milk
1 tbsp. chopped sweet pickle
1 tbsp. chopped toasted almonds
1/4 tsp. salt

Serve with baked or broiled fish.

Mom's Helpers

Cooking rice will not boil over if a small lump of butter is added to the pot.

To give pates or meat loaves added pizzazz, add a dash or more of powdered allspice.

To make oven cleaning really simple, just put a bowl of ammonia in it, close the door, and leave overnight. Baked on grease and grime will wash off easily in the morning. Keep the kitchen well ventilated while washing off the ammonia.

TOMATO CURRIED COD

2 lbs. cod
1 cup chopped spanish onion
$^1/_2$ clove garlic, minced
3 tbsp. butter
$^3/_4$ cup water
1 can (6 oz.) tomato paste
1 tsp. salt
1 tsp. curry powder
Pepper
3 medium apples, quartered

Cut cod into serving pieces and poach until it flakes easily (approx. 10 minutes per one-inch thickness of fish). Cook onion and garlic in butter until tender. Add water, tomato paste, salt, curry powder, pepper, and apple quarters. Cook gently until apple is tender. Spoon sauce over cooked fish and serve. Serves 6.

WESTERN SHRIMP FAVOURITE

1 lb. cooked shrimp
$^1/_2$ cup finely chopped onion
1 clove finely chopped garlic
$1^1/_2$ tbsp. butter
1 tsp. turmeric
1 tsp. coriander
$^1/_2$ cup water
1 tbsp. brown sugar
2 tbsp. white vinegar or lemon juice
Salt to taste

Cook onion and garlic in butter until tender. Add turmeric, coriander, water, brown sugar, vinegar or lemon juice, and salt. Bring to a boil. Add shrimp and simmer gently for 10 minutes. Serve with rice. Makes 4-6 servings.

Mom's Helpers

Prevent fat from spattering when you are frying by sprinkling salt in the skillet before you add any fat or food.

Place a peel of an orange into the brown sugar container. As long as there is moisture in the peel, the brown sugar will remain soft. When the peel dries out entirely, replace with a new one. A peel will last for weeks.

APPETIZER SPARERIBS

Simmer the ribs ahead. Glaze just before serving.
Cut 2½ lbs. spareribs in 2-inch pieces, place in pot. Add 2 tbsp. minced onion and 2 tsp. salt. Cover with water. Simmer covered until meat is tender, about 45 minutes. Drain and chill. Prepare the following sauce when ready to serve:

Sparerib Sauce:

> 1 beef cube or 1½ beef bouillon powder
> ¾ cup boiling water
> 2 tbsp. cornstarch
> ¼ cup cider vinegar
> 2 tbsp. soy sauce
> ¾ cup brown sugar
> ½ tsp. each ginger, garlic powder
> ¼ tsp. cloves

Dissolve beef cubes or powder in boiling water. Stir in cornstarch mixed with vinegar. Add remaining ingredients and cook stirring constantly until sauce thickens. Add spareribs and cook until glazed and heated thoroughly. If desired, ribs may be glazed by baking in 375 degree F. oven for about ½ hour. Serve with prepared horseradish mustard and plum sauce.

Horseradish Sauce:

> 1 onion cube
> ½ cup boiling water
> ¾ cup chili sauce or catsup
> 2 tbsp. horseradish (fresh or commercially prepared)
> 1 tsp. lemon juice
> ½ tsp. Worcestershire sauce
> 1½ tsp. dry mustard

Dissolve the onion cube in boiling water. Combine with remaining ingredients and blend thoroughly. Keeps well.

Plum Sauce:

> 1 chicken cube
> ½ cup boiling water
> 1 cup plum or apricot jam
> ¼ cup brown sugar
> ¼ tsp. ground allspice
> ½ tsp. ginger

Dissolve chicken cube in ½ cup boiling water. Mix remaining ingredients in a saucepan, add chicken cube. Heat, stirring constantly until boiling and allow to simmer for 10 minutes.

BARBECUED RIBS IN SAUCE

3 lbs. beef ribs, cut into serving pieces
2 tbsp. fat
1 chopped onion
$^1/_4$ cup vinegar
2 tbsp. sugar
1 cup catsup
$^1/_2$ cup water
2 tbsp. Worcestershire sauce
1 tsp. prepared mustard
$^1/_2$ cup sliced celery
1 to $1^1/_2$ tsp. salt

Melt fat in heavy skillet. Brown the ribs with the onions in hot fat. Add all the remaining ingredients. Cover and cook slowly 2 to $2^1/_2$ hours on top of the stove, or place in a roasting pan, cover, and bake in a moderate oven 350 degrees F., basting occasionally, for 2-3 hours.

BARBECUED SHORT RIBS

$^1/_4$ cup flour
3 lbs. short ribs, cut into serving pieces
2 tbsp. fat
1 cup chili sauce
1 cup water
$^1/_4$ cup vinegar
1 medium sized onion, finely chopped
$^1/_2$ cup finely diced celery
2 to 3 tsp. Worcestershire sauce
1 tsp. salt
$^1/_4$ tsp. dry mustard

Place flour in a sturdy paper bag. Coat short ribs with flour by shaking them in the bag. Melt fat in large skillet over low heat; add floured short ribs to hot fat. Cook over low to moderate heat, turning short ribs until they are well browned on all sides. Pour off fat. Combine chili sauce, water, vinegar, onion, celery, Worcestershire sauce, mustard and salt. Mix well and pour over browned short ribs. Bring to boiling point, then lower heat to 275 degrees F. and cook slowly for about 2 hours or until tender.
Add more salt if necessary, and a teaspoon or two of sugar. Serve atop buttered rice. Serves 4.

Mom's Helpers
To thicken sauces, 1 whole egg, 2 yolks, or 2 whites can replace 1 tbsp. of flour or 2 tsp. of cornstarch.

Golden Rice Salad, Page 51, Pineapple Almond Chicken, Page 36

BEEF CURRY

$1^1/_2$ lbs. beef round steak, cut in $^3/_4$ inch cubes
     Flour, salt, pepper
  2 tbsp. shortening
  1 diced medium onion
$^1/_2$ clove finely minced garlic
  1 beef bouillon cube
  1 cup boiling water
  1 to 2 tsp. curry powder
$^1/_2$ cup tomato juice
  2 tbsp. flour

Dredge beef in seasoned flour. Melt shortening and brown meat. Add onion and garlic and brown lightly. Reduce heat. Dissolve bouillon in water; add curry powder and pour over meat. Cover and cook 1 hour or until tender. Combine tomato juice and flour. Add to meat and cook to thicken.

BEEF LIVER WITH APPLES AND ONIONS

$1^1/_2$ lb. beef liver sliced $^1/_4$ inch thick
  6 slices bacon, cut into 1 inch pieces
$^1/_2$ cup flour
$^1/_2$ tsp. salt
  1 tsp. thyme
$^1/_8$ tsp. pepper
  2 tbsp. lemon juice
  2 medium red skinned apples, diced
  1 large onion, sliced
  2 tbsp. chopped parsley

Pan fry bacon until partially cooked. Combine flour, salt, thyme and pepper. Dip liver slices into the flour mixture. Brown liver on both sides in the bacon drippings. Combine lemon juice with apples. Add apples, onions and parsley to skillet. Cover. Cook over low heat 20 minutes. Serves 6.

Mom's Helpers

For further inflation of popovers, add an extra egg white to the batter.

Rub chicken, pork, or lamb with curry powder before roasting. Use anywhere from one to two teaspoons, depending on the size of the roast and whether you want a pronounced curry flavour or a subtle, but delicious, taste.

BROILED BARBECUED CHICKEN

1¹/₂ cups tomato juice
 ¹/₄ tsp. pepper
 ¹/₄ tsp. dry mustard
   2 tbsp. Worcestershire sauce
   3 tbsp. vinegar
 ¹/₄ cup shortening
   2 green onions, finely chopped
   2 fryer chickens

Place 2 fryer chickens, halved, on broiler pan. Skin side down so top surface of chicken is 4 inches from heat. Broil 10 minutes. Turn and brush with sauce. Broil for 10 minutes. Reduce heat, brush chicken with sauce frequently and broil for another 30-35 minutes.

BROILED OR BARBECUED SPARERIBS

   3 lbs. back or side pork ribs, cut into serving pieces
 ¹/₂ cup honey
 ¹/₄ cup pineapple juice
   2 tbsp. soya sauce
 ¹/₄ tsp. ground ginger
   1 finely crushed clove of garlic

Cover ribs with boiling water and simmer until almost tender. Drain. Combine remaining ingredients and heat. Broil or barbecue ribs, basting frequently with sauce. Serves 4 to 5.

CHICKEN CACCIATORE

   2 lbs. frying chicken
 ¹/₄ cup olive oil
   2 medium onions, minced
   1 clove garlic, minced
   2 green peppers, minced
   2 red peppers, minced
1¹/₂ cups canned tomatoes
   1 6-oz. can tomato paste

Brown the chicken in olive oil until golden brown. Add all but the last two ingredients and cook until vegetables are cooked. Add tomatoes and paste to chicken mixture. Cover and cook for approx. 30 minutes or until the chicken is tender. Serve with spaghetti if desired. Serves 6.

CHICKEN WITH WINE SAUCE

$1^1/_2$ tbsp. flour
$^1/_2$ salt
$^1/_2$ tsp. pepper
  2 large chicken breasts, deboned and skinned
  4 tbsp. butter
$^1/_2$ lb. thinly sliced mushrooms
$^1/_4$ cup chopped onion
$^1/_4$ cup chopped parsley
  1 cup white wine

Combine flour, salt and pepper. Coat chicken with mixture. Reserve excess flour. Melt 2 tbsp. butter in large saucepan over medium heat. Brown chicken. Remove from pan. Add remaining butter, mushrooms, onion, and 2 tbsp. chopped parsley; saute for 1 minute. Remove from heat; stir in reserved flour. Blend in wine. Bring to a boil, stirring steadily. Add chicken. Cover, reduce heat and simmer for 30-45 minutes untill chicken is tender.

CHINESE SPARERIBS

  2 lbs. pork spareribs
$1^1/_2$ tsp. salt
    Boiling water
  2 tbsp. shortening
  2 tbsp. bouillon mix
  2 tbsp. cornstarch
  3 tbsp. brown sugar
  1 tbsp. soy sauce
$^1/_3$ cup vinegar
$^3/_4$ cup cold water
  1 can (approx. 20 oz.) pineapple chunks
  1 onion, thinly sliced
$^1/_2$ green pepper, cut into thin strips
  1 cup sliced celery

Cut ribs into single pieces. Add salt and cover with boiling water; simmer, covered, until pork is almost tender, about 1 hour. Drain thoroughly. Heat shortening or cooking oil; add cooked spareribs and brown on all sides. Combine bouillon, cornstarch, brown sugar, soy sauce, vinegar, the $^3/_4$ cup cold water and syrup drained from pineapple; pour over spareribs. Cook, stirring constantly, until sauce comes to a boil. Add onion, green pepper, celery and pineapple. Cover and simmer until vegetables are crisply tender — about 10 minutes.

CHINESE VEGETABLES WITH BEEF

$^1/_2$ lb. round steak or leftover beef roast
1 tbsp. soya sauce
1 tsp. sugar
4 cups fresh vegetables, cut into strips (mushrooms, green beans, zucchini, carrots, peas, celery, etc.)
2 tbsp. oil
$^1/_4$ tsp. salt
2 tsp. cornstarch mixed with $^1/_4$ cup water or broth

Cut meat into strips (approx. 1$^1/_2$ cups meat). Combine soya sauce and sugar. Pour over meat and allow meat to marinate for 30 minutes. Cut vegetables on the diagonal into strips. (Four different vegetables make a nice combination — 1 cup each). Parboil carrots and fresh green beans by dropping them into boiling water for 1-2 minutes. Drain and cool. Heat oil and salt in frypan on high heat. Add meat and cook for 2-3 minutes until well browned. Add vegetables and stir fry for 2-3 minutes. Add cornstarch and water mixture and cook until thick. Serve immediately. Serves 4.

CORNED BEEF

5-6 lb. brisket of beef
$^1/_2$ tsp. saltpeter
$^1/_4$ cup warm water
2$^1/_2$ tbsp. brown sugar
2 cloves crushed garlic
1$^1/_2$ tbsp. pickling spice
1 cup salt dissolved in 2 quarts water

Dissolve saltpeter in $^1/_4$ cup warm water. Mix in the remaining ingredients, except beef, to form a brine. Place the beef in a large glass container or crock and pour the brine over the beef. Cover the beef and weight it down so that the beef is covered in brine continually. Let beef and brine stand in cool place or fridge for 3 weeks, turning occasionally.

2 quarts cold water
4 bay leaves
1 tsp. cloves
1 sliced onion

Remove beef from the brine and place into a large pot. Mix bay leaves, cloves and onion with cold water. Pour mixture over the beef. Bring to a boil and simmer gently until the meat is tender — about 1 hour per pound. When done, chill and slice as desired. Cross rib or beef tongue could be used instead of brisket.

CORNISH HEN WILD RICE STUFFING

1 cup raw wild rice
$^1/_2$ cup chopped onion
$^1/_2$ lb. mushrooms, sliced
1 cup shaved filberts
1 cup orange sections (optional)
6 tbsp. butter
$^1/_2$ tsp. marjoram
$^1/_2$ tsp. thyme

Wash rice and simmer in 3 cups boiling water covered with 1 tsp. salt, for 50 minutes. Drain. Saute onions, mushrooms, filberts in the butter until limp but not brown. Add orange if used. Add seasonings. Stir and add to rice. This yields 3$^1/_2$ cups stuffing — enough for 6 hens. Sprinkle cavities of hens with salt and stuff and truss them. Place two one-half slices bacon over each bird and roast, uncovered, at 350 dgrees F. for 1$^1/_2$ hours until tender. Baste with pan drippings to which you have added the 2 tbsp. butter. Do not overbake so that birds will hold their shape when served.

CURRIED CHICKEN

3 to 3$^1/_2$ lb. chicken
Flour
2 tbsp. shortening
1 cup water
$^1/_2$ cup onions
1$^1/_2$ tsp. curry powder
$^1/_8$ tsp. marjoram
$^3/_4$ tsp. salt
$^1/_8$ tsp. pepper

Cut chicken into serving pieces, dredge in flour. Melt shortening and brown chicken on all sides. Lower heat. Combine water, onions, curry, marjoram, salt and pepper and pour over chicken. Cover and cook until tender, adding more liquid if necessary.

Mom's Helpers

Labeling of frozen foods helps in finding them and in using first those that have been in the freezer the longest.

Guard against too hot a curry sauce by starting with half the amount a recipe calls for. You can always add more later. Different brands of curry vary enormously in flavour and strength.

CURRIED CHICKEN CASSEROLE

2 eggs, beaten
1/4 cup light cream
2 cups cream style corn
3 cups diced cooked chicken
1/2 cup raisins
1/2 tsp. salt
1/2 to 1 tsp. curry powder (according to taste)

Blend eggs with cream and corn. Mix in remaining ingredients. Spoon into a greased 2-quart casserole. Cover and bake in slow oven 325 degrees F. for about 45 minutes. Garnish with crisp bacon bits. Serves 4 to 6.

FAMILY MEAT LOAF

1 1/2 lb. ground beef
1/4 cup diced onion
1 cup uncooked oatmeal
1/4 cup catsup
1 tsp. salt
1/4 tsp. pepper
1 tsp. dry mustard
1 egg mixed with 1 cup milk

Topping:

1/4 cup catsup
1/4 tsp. nutmeg
3 tbsp. brown sugar
1 tsp. dry mustard

Mix all ingredients together in 6-8 cup casserole dish. Spread topping and bake uncovered. Bake one hour at 375 degrees F.

Mom's Helpers

To tenderize a steak, brush it on both sides with lime juice several hours before cooking it.

When serving a buffet for a large crowd, and your salad bowls and platters are not large enough, cover both halves of an oval or round roasting pan with foil and use for salad. A foil covered tray makes a good platter for cold meats.

FANTASTIC COUNTRY PIE

Crust:

- $^1/_2$ cup canned tomato soup
- $^3/_4$ cup bread crumbs
- $^1/_3$ cup chopped onion
- $^3/_4$ tsp. salt
- $^1/_8$ tsp. pepper
- $^1/_8$ tsp. oregano
- 1 lb. ground beef
- $^1/_4$ cup chopped green pepper

Combine all ingredients, mix well, and pat meat mixture into a greased 9-inch pie plate. Set aside.

Filling:

- $1^1/_3$ cups minute rice
- $1^1/_2$ cups tomato sauce
- 1 cup water
- $^1/_2$ tsp. salt
- $^1/_8$ tsp. oregano
- 1 cup grated yellow cheese

Combine rice, sauce, salt, water and $^1/_4$ cup of cheese. Spoon into meat shell. Cover with aluminum foil. Bake in 350 degrees F. for 30-35 minutes. Uncover and sprinkle top with remaining cheese. Return to oven and bake 10 minutes longer. Serves 5-6.

HELEN'S WESTERN SURPRISE

- $^1/_2$ cup chopped onion, packed
- 1 cup chopped celery
- 2 cups chopped weiners
- 2 cups canned brown beans
- $^1/_4$ cup molasses
- $^1/_4$ cup brown sugar
- $^1/_4$ cup water
- 1 tsp. butter
- $1^1/_2$ tsp. powdered gravy mix
- 1 tsp. curry powder
- $^1/_2$ tsp. maple flavouring
- $^1/_4$ tsp. dry mustard

Mix molasses, brown sugar, water, butter, gravy mix, and curry powder in $1^1/_2$ quart saucepan. Add onions and celery and place over heat and cook for 1 minute. Add brown beans, weiners, and mustard and cook for another 2 minutes. Add flavouring. Serves 4.

HAWAIIAN MEATBALLS

1¹/₂ lbs. ground beef
¹/₃ cup minced onion
1¹/₂ tsp. salt
¹/₄ cup milk
¹/₂ cup brown sugar
¹/₃ cup vinegar
1 tbsp. soya sauce
²/₃ cup cracker crumbs
1 egg
¹/₄ tsp. ginger
1 tbsp. cornstarch
1 20 oz. can of pineapple chunks and juice
1 cup chopped green pepper

Mix beef, crumbs, onion, egg, salt, ginger, and milk. Shape into small meatballs. Heat oil in large skillet and cook meatballs. Remove from fry pan and drain fat from pan. Mix cornstarch and sugar, stir in pineapple syrup, vinegar and soya sauce, mix until smooth. Pour into skillet, cook over medium heat, stirring until thick and boils. Boil 1 minute. Stir continuously. Add meatballs, green pepper and pineapple chunks and heat through. Serve hot with steamed rice. Serves 6.

INDIVIDUAL ITALIAN MEAT LOAVES

³/₄ cup medium cracker crumbs
1 cup milk
1¹/₂ lb. ground beef
2 eggs
¹/₂ cup grated Romano cheese
¹/₄ cup green minced pepper
¹/₄ cup minced onion
1 tbsp. Worcestershire sauce
¹/₂ tsp. salt
¹/₂ tsp. garlic salt
¹/₄ tsp. basil
Dash pepper
Catsup

Soak cracker crumbs in milk; add remaining ingredients except catsup; mix well. Shape in 6 individual loaves; place in shallow baking pan or jelly roll pan. Spread catsup over loaves; sprinkle with a small amount of additional Romano cheese and basil. Bake at 350 degrees F. for 45 minutes.

IRISH STEW

  2 lbs. boneless stewing lamb
  2 tbsp. fat
1¹/₂ cups sliced onion
  1 crushed clove of garlic
  2 tsp. salt
 ¹/₄ cup flour
    Dash of pepper
 ¹/₄ tsp. thyme
2³/₄ cup water
  6 medium carrots, cut into 1 inch pieces
  6 medium potatoes, cut into 1 inch pieces

Trim excess fat from meat and cut into 1-inch pieces. Brown meat in fat and remove from pan. Add onion and garlic and saute until onion is transparent. Return meat to pan, sprinkle with flour and brown again lightly. Cover and simmer until meat is almost tender (³/₄ to 1 hour). Add vegetables and cook until tender — about 30 to 45 minutes. Serves 6.

LAMB AND BARLEY STEW

  1 tbsp. butter
  2 lbs. lamb shoulder, cut into 2-inch cubes
  4 cups hot water
 ¹/₂ cup pearl barley
  1 medium sized onion, thinly sliced
  3 carrots, diced
  1 small turnip, diced
  1 tsp. salt
 ¹/₄ tsp. pepper
 ¹/₄ cup finely chopped parsley
  1 bay leaf

Melt butter in large heavy saucepan over low heat; add cubed lamb to hot butter. Cook over low to medium heat, turning lamb cubes until they are well browned on all sides. Stir in water and barley and mix well. Increase heat and bring contents of saucepan to the boiling point. Then lower heat, cover saucepan and simmer lamb slowly for about 2 hours or until meat is tender. Add onion, carrots, turnip, salt, pepper, parsley and bay leaf. Cover saucepan and continue simmering for about 30 minutes or until vegetables and lamb are tender. Remove bay leaf. If necessary, thicken stew with a little flour and cold water blended together in equal parts. Serve over buttered toast. Serves 6.

LAMB CURRY SPECIAL

2 lbs. cubed shoulder of lamb
3 tbsp. shortening
1 cup chopped onions
2 tbsp. flour
1 tsp. salt
$^1/_2$ tsp. dry mustard
1 tbsp. curry powder
$^1/_2$ tsp. sugar
2 cups water
1 tbsp. lemon juice
1 tart apple, peeled and diced
2 tbsp. seedless raisins

Melt shortening in large pan and saute onions until lightly browned. Dredge meat in combined flour, salt, mustard, curry powder and sugar mixture and place in pan. Increase heat and brown on both sides. Add water, lemon juice, apple and raisins. Lower heat, cover pan and braise until tender.

LIVER PATE

1 lb. pork liver
$^1/_2$ lb. fresh pork fat
1 large onion
2-3 tsp. salt
$^1/_2$ tsp. pepper
$^1/_4$ tsp. allspice
$^1/_4$ tsp. ginger
$^1/_8$ tsp. nutmeg
2 eggs, separated
$^1/_2$ cup light cream

With a fine blade in the grinder (a food processor can be used), grind the liver, pork fat and onion. Add seasonings and cream to beaten egg yolks. Combine egg mixture and ground ingredients. Fold in stiffly beaten egg whites. Pour into a greased 9 × 5 inch loaf pan. Cover pan with foil and place in a pan of hot water in the oven. Bake in a slow oven at 300 degrees F. for $1^1/_2$ to 2 hours. Allow to cook and refrigerate until serving time.

Mom's Helpers

When preparing steaks or chops for freezing, place strips of the paper wrappers from margarine or butter between the pieces of meat. When frozen, the pieces separate quickly with a knife blade.

Panbroil without fat: Heat a heavy skillet, sprinkle salt over the bottom, add meat and cook to the level desired.

LASAGNA

6 cups Meat Sauce (recipe follows)
12 lasagna noodles, cooked and drained
Bechamel sauce with Parmesan cheese (recipe follows)
$^1/_2$ cup grated Parmesan cheese

Spread I cup Meat Sauce in $12 \times 8 \times 2$-inch baking dish. Place 3 noodles for each layer (trim if necessary to fit your pan). Spread $1^1/_3$ cups Bechamel Sauce over the layer, then place three noodles, then spread $2^1/_2$ cups Meat Sauce and $^1/_4$ cup Parmesan. Repeat layers with remaining ingredients. Cover loosely with foil. Bake in preheated 375 degree F. oven 45 minutes. Remove foil, and bake 15 minutes longer until bubbly and lightly browned around the edges. For easy cutting, let stand 10 to 15 minutes. Serves 8.

Meat Sauce:

$^1/_2$ cup each finely chopped onion and carrot
$^1/_3$ cup finely chopped celery
$^1/_4$ cup olive oil
3 tbsp. butter
1 lb. ground lean beef
1 cup each dry red or white wine and milk
1 tsp. salt
1 tsp. pepper
$^1/_8$ tsp. nutmeg
4 cups canned tomatoes, put through a sieve or blender
1 6-oz. can tomato paste
1 tbsp. dried basil

In large saucepan, saute onion, carrot and celery in oil and butter for 5 minutes. Add beef and cook, stirring to break up, until brown (about 6 minutes). Add wine and cook over medium heat about 3-4 minutes. Stir in milk, salt, pepper and nutmeg. Cook and stir for 2 minutes. Add tomatoes, tomato paste and basil. Stir to blend well. Bring to boil then reduce heat and simmer uncovered, for about 1 hour or until thick. Makes 9 cups. Extra sauce can be used for a spaghetti meal.

Bechamel Sauce:

$^1/_4$ cup butter
$^1/_4$ cup flour
$^1/_4$ tsp. salt
$2^1/_2$ cups milk
$^1/_2$ cup grated Parmesan cheese

In small saucepan over medium heat melt butter, stir in flour and salt until smooth. Gradually stir in milk. Cook and stir 6 to 8 minutes or until thick. Add cheese and stir 2 minutes or until cheese melts. Makes $2^3/_4$ cups.

MAPLE-BAKED SPARERIBS

Baking spareribs keeps them juicy and moist; this sauce makes them taste as though they have been barbecued.

        3 lbs. spareribs
      3/4 cup maple syrup
        1 tbsp. catsup
        1 tbsp. cider vinegar
        1 tbsp. finely chopped onion
        1 tsp. dry mustard

Cut spareribs into serving-size pieces and simmer in water just to cover, for about 30 minutes. Drain. Mix remaining ingredients together. Put spareribs in shallow baking pan and pour half the sauce over. Bake at 350 degrees F. turning and basting with remaining sauce. If not brown enough, coat with sauce and place under the broiler for a few minutes. Serves 4 to 5.

MEAL-IN-ONE-LIVER

        1 lb. sliced liver dusted with flour
        3 tbsp. fat
        3 thinly sliced raw potatoes
        1 cup sliced onions
    1 1/2 cups white sauce

Dip liver in flour; brown in fat. Cut liver into 1-inch cubes. Saute potatoes and onion in fat until brown and tender. Alternate with layers of liver in baking dish. Add white sauce and bake in moderate oven 20 minutes. Serves 4.

White Sauce:

        2 tbsp. butter
        2 tbsp. flour
        1 cup milk
      1/4 tsp. salt
      1/4 tsp. pepper

Melt butter in a heavy skillet. Add flour and stir until well blended. Stir in milk very slowly and continue stirring. Add salt and pepper. Cook on slow heat until sauce is smooth and thick and comes to a boil.

Mom's Helpers
Tenderize a tough piece of pot roast with tomatoes. Add the tomatoes — fresh or canned — to the usual vegetables and seasonings with which you cook the meat. The acid in the tomatoes helps break down the tough fibers of the meat.

MEAT AND POTATO PIE

1 can condensed cream of potato soup (10 oz.)
2 beef bouillon cubes
$^1/_2$ cup boiling water
1 lb. ground chuck
1 finely chopped onion
$^1/_2$ tsp. pepper
1 small egg, whipped
Pastry for 1 2-crust pie

In a medium-sized bowl dissolve bouillon cubes in boiling water and blend in the soup. Mix in meat, onion, and pepper. (Extra salt is not necessary) Roll out half the pastry and line a 9-inch pie plate. Trim. Roll out top crust. Turn meat mixture into pastry-lined pie plate. Cover with a top crust. Brush top crust with whipped egg. Seal the edges and slit the top to allow steam to escape. Bake in preheated 425 degree F. oven for 10 to 15 minutes or until pastry is golden. Reduce heat to 350 degrees F. and continue baking for one hour. Serve hot or cold. Keeps well in foil wrap in refrigerator. Serves 5 to 6.

ORIENTAL BEEF AND GREENS

$^1/_4$ cup peanut oil
$^1/_4$ cup sherry
$^1/_4$ cup soya sauce
1 clove garlic, crushed
$^1/_2$ tsp. minced fresh ginger
$1^1/_2$ lbs. beef round, cut in 2 × $^1/_2$ inch pieces
5 tbsp. peanut oil
2 cups celery, diagonally sliced
2 cups carrots, diagonally sliced
2 cups bok choy, diagonally sliced
1 cup sliced mushrooms
1 cup beef stock
$^1/_4$ cup sliced water chestnuts
2 tbsp. cornstarch

Mix well together the $^1/_4$ cup peanut oil, sherry, soya sauce, garlic, and ginger. Pour over sliced beef. Marinate in refrigerator 1 to 2 hours. In a large saucepan heat 3 tbsp. peanut oil. Brown meat, reserving marinade. Set aside. Add 1 tbsp. oil to pan. Saute celery, carrots, and bok choy until celery turns bright green. Remove from heat and set aside. Pour 1 tbsp. peanut oil into pan. Saute mushrooms until golden. Add reserved marinade, beef stock, beef, celery, bok choy and carrots. Bring to a boil. Reduce heat, cover and simmer 15 minutes or until beef is tender. Stir in water chestnuts. Combine cornstarch with a little broth until smooth; stir into hot broth. Cook until thick. Serve with cooked rice.

OLD FASHIONED BREAD AND CELERY STUFFING

    2 cups diced celery
    1 cup chopped onion
  3/4 cup butter
    8 cups dry bread crumbs
1 1/2 tsp. salt
    2 tsp. poultry seasoning
  1/2 tsp. sage
  1/2 tsp. pepper
    1 cup water
1 1/2 cups raisins (optional)

Cook celery and onion in butter over medium heat until onion is transparent but not brown; stir occasionally. Combine seasonings with bread crumbs and toss together. Add water and onion mixture. Add raisins if desired. This makes enough stuffing for a 14 to 18 lb. bird. (This is a moist stuffing that holds its shape and scoops out very nicely with an ice cream scoop.)

PINEAPPLE ALMOND CHICKEN

    2 lbs. chicken sliced
    1 20 oz. tin pineapple cubes and juice
    2 tbsp. brown sugar
  1/4 cup brown vinegar
1 1/2 tsp. salt
       Peanut oil
  1/2 cup toasted almonds
       Flour
  3/4 cup water

Fry the chicken in the peanut oil for a few minutes. In a large saucepan mix pineapple juice, brown sugar, vinegar, water and salt. Let cook for a few minutes. In another saucepan, put 5 tbsp. of oil, then slowly stir in 4 tbsp. flour. Add to pineapple mixture stirring well. Add chicken to sauce mixture and let simmer for 1 1/2 hours, until meat is tender. Sprinkle with almonds and serve. Serves 4.

Mom's Helpers

To keep rice snowy white and grains separate, add a few drops of lemon juice to the water when it is cooking.

To make the juiciest hamburgers, add 1/3 cup of applesauce for each pound of meat, add salt and pepper, shape the meat into patties and cook as usual.

PORK CHOPS WITH CARAWAY SEED

4 to 6 pork chops
  Flour
1 egg, slightly beaten
  Fine cracker crumbs
2 tbsp. shortening
1 cup water or tomato juice
1 tsp. caraway seed
$^1/_2$ tsp. salt
$^1/_8$ tsp. pepper

Dredge chops in flour. Dip in beaten egg, then in cracker crumbs. Melt shortening and brown chops on both sides. Reduce heat. Add liquid, caraway seed, salt and pepper. Cover and braise until well done, adding more liquid if necessary.

SAVORY VEAL CHOPS

6 veal chops
2 tbsp. shortening
$^1/_2$ tsp. salt
$^1/_4$ tsp. pepper
1 cup water or beef bouillon
$^1/_8$ tsp. basil
$^1/_8$ tsp. marjoram

Melt shortening and brown chops on both sides, season with salt and pepper. Reduce heat. Combine water or bouillon, basil, and marjoram with $^1/_4$ cup of water. Add to chops. Simmer for 3 minutes, then add remaining liquid slowly, cover and braise until done.

SPICED BEEF TONGUE

1 4-lb. beef tongue
2 tsp. salt
3 bay leaves
6 whole allspice
3 whole black peppercorns
1 medium onion, sliced
2 carrots, sliced
1 cup diced celery and leaves

Wash tongue. Cover with hot water, then add seasonings and vegetables. Simmer for 3 to 4 hours. Cool in liquid. Trim excess tissue from root, and remove skin and cartilage. Slice and serve hot with potato salad. Serves 6 to 8. Tongue slices very nicely when chilled.

SPECIAL PEPPER STEAK

$1/4$ cup soya sauce
1 tbsp. water
$1^1/2$ tsp. cornstarch
$1/4$ tsp. pepper
2 cloves garlic, crushed
1 lb. round steak
2 tbsp. margarine
2 large tomatoes, cut in wedges
$2^1/2$ cups diced green peppers (1-inch pieces)

In medium sized bowl, blend together soya sauce, water, cornstarch, pepper and garlic. Thinly slice steak on an angle across the grain. Mix into soya sauce mixture. Let mixture sit for an hour before frying. Melt margarine in a large fry pan. Add peppers and saute — stir — add tomatoes. Mix in meat and soya mixture. Cook, stirring until meat loses its red color, about 5-6 minutes. Serves 4.

SPICY BARBECUE SAUCE

$3/4$ cup catsup
$1/2$ cup water
$1/4$ cup olive oil
$3/4$ cup minced onion
3 tsp. brown sugar
2 tbsp. Worcestershire sauce
$1/4$ cup vinegar
2 tsp. salt
1 bay leaf
2 tbsp. mustard seed
1 tsp. coarse black pepper
$1/2$ tsp. cloves
1 tsp. chili powder
2 tsp. paprika

Blend dry ingredients and add to liquids. Simmer for one hour over low heat. Makes about 2 cups.

Mom's Helpers

To give cooked mushrooms a rich dark brown color, saute them in butter over high heat and use a black iron skillet.

Insert a toothpick into a clove of garlic or a small piece of fresh ginger root when either is to be removed at the end of the cooking period. It makes either one so much easier to locate.

Cream of Leek Soup, Page 48, Egg Drop Soup
Page 45, Borsch, Page 42

STANDING RIB ROAST

6-8 lb. standing rib roast
$^1/_3$ tsp. salt
$^1/_3$ tsp. pepper

Preheat oven to 325 degrees F. In open roasting pan place the roast, fat side up, on rib bones. Sprinkle with salt and pepper. Test for readiness with a meat thermometer. When done place on cutting board and let stand for 15 minutes for easier carving. Serve with Yorkshire Pudding and Horseradish. Garnish roast with canned crab apples and parsley.

STROGANOFF CASSEROLE

1 lb. round steak
2 tbsp. flour
2 cups canned sweet peas, with liquid
$^1/_2$ cup thick sour cream
$^1/_2$ tsp. salt
4 oz. of thin noodles, cooked and drained
1 cup of canned mushrooms

Cut steak in long thin strips and brown in a small amount of melted shortening in a heavy frying pan. Stir in flour; add liquid from peas. Cook until thick and smooth. Remove from heat, mix in peas and remaining ingredients. Pour into a 2-quart casserole dish and bake at 325 degrees F. for 40 minutes. Serves 4 to 6.

SWEET 'N' SOUR SPARE RIBS

3 lbs. pork ribs
1 tbsp. shortening
1 minced clove garlic
$^1/_4$ tsp. ginger
$^1/_4$ tsp. pepper
$^3/_4$ tsp salt
$^1/_2$ cup brown sugar
$^1/_2$ cup vinegar
2 tbsp. soya sauce

Melt shortening and cook ribs until browned. Lower heat. Combine garlic, ginger, salt, pepper, sugar, vinegar and soya sauce and pour over ribs. Cover and braise 1$^1/_2$ hours or until tender and ribs are glazed.

STUFFED GREEN PEPPERS

    4 large green peppers
    1 lb. ground beef chuck
    3 cups stewed tomatoes with liquid
    1 cup cooked rice
  $2/3$ cup wheat bran cereal
  $1/2$ tsp. salt
  $1/4$ tsp. oregano leaves
  $1/4$ tsp. basil leaves
  $1/8$ tsp. ground black pepper
  $1/2$ cup sliced onion
    1 cup sliced zucchini

Cut tops from peppers and reserve. Remove seeds and stems. Cook peppers and tops in boiling salted water for 5 minutes; drain. Brown beef well; drain off excess fat. Add 1 cup tomatoes, rice, cereal and seasonings to meat; blend well. Spoon into peppers and replace tops. Pour remaining stewed tomatoes into a large skillet or Dutch oven. Place peppers in sauce and surround with onions. Cover and simmer for 30 minutes. Add zucchini; cook 10 to 15 minutes longer, or until peppers and zucchini are tender. Serve with cheese, if desired. Serves 4.

TOMATOES AND CHEESE WITH LIVER

    1 lb. beef liver
  $2^1/4$ cups canned tomatoes
    1 cup sliced onion
    1 tsp. salt
    1 tsp. sugar
  $1/2$ to 1 tsp. Worcestershire sauce
  $1/4$ tsp. basil
    1 cup cheddar cheese, grated
    1 tbsp. butter

Wash liver and remove membrane. Cut into serving size pieces. Brown with onions in butter. Add tomatoes and seasonings. Simmer 15 minutes. Add cheese. Stir until melted. Serves 4.

Mom's Helpers

Prevent sausages from bursting open and spattering fat while they cook by piercing the skins frequently with a fork while the sausages are cooking.

KITCHEN KETTLE

SOUPS and SALADS

BEEFY BORSCH

  3 medium beets
  8 cups cold water
     Juice and grated peel of 1 lemon
  1 lb. ground beef
  1 egg, beaten
  1 small onion, grated
  1 tsp. salt
 1/4 tsp. pepper
  6 medium potatoes, peeled

Scrub the beets thoroughly, but do not peel them. Place in a saucepan and add the water and lemon juice, cover and boil gently for about 1 hour. Beets should be tender. Remove the beets from the stock and let them cool. Reserve the stock. Peel the beets, then grate them over the stock and bring to a boil.

In a separate bowl, combine ground beef, beaten egg, onion, salt and pepper. Blend well, shape into 12 small meatballs and drop into the boiling stock. Add the potatoes to the stock, then cover and simmer for 30 minutes or until the potatoes are done.

When serving, place 2 meatballs and 1 potato in each bowl and ladle the soup over them. Serves 6.

BORSCH

 1/2 lb. lean beef, minced or diced
 1/2 cup carrots, shredded
  1 cup onion, finely chopped
  2 cups fresh beets, grated
  1 cup cabbage, shredded
  1 cup tomatoes, canned
  3 cups beef stock
  1 tbsp. vinegar or lemon juice
     Salt and pepper to taste

Lightly saute beef, carrot, onion and beets in 2 tbsp. butter. Add tomatoes, stock and vinegar or lemon juice, cover and simmer for 1 hour. Add shredded cabbage and cook for further ten minutes, then season to taste. Minced, fresh garlic, as you like it, can be included with the vegetables. Serves 6.

Mom's Helpers

To prepare meat, fish, or vegetable stock for freezing, boil the stock — uncovered — until it has cooked down to 1/4 or 1/2 of the original quantity, then freeze it. This takes up much less storage space. The stock can be reconstituted easily by adding liquid when you are ready to use it.

COUNTRY BEAN SOUP

1 ham bone or 2 thin ham steaks, diced
1 cup chopped celery
1 large onion, diced
3 carrots, thinly sliced
1 tbsp. salt
$^1/_2$ tsp. pepper
1 cup tomato juice
1 lb. dried navy beans
3 quarts cold water

Wash the beans and place them in a large saucepan. Cover with the cold water and let stand overnight to soak. Next morning, bring the beans to a fast rolling boil over high heat. Add the ham bone or substitute, cover and simmer over low heat for 2 to 3 hours. Add the remaining ingredients and simmer, covered, for 1 more hour. Makes about 3 quarts.

CREAM OF CABBAGE SOUP

1 onion, chopped
2 carrots, diced
2 celery stalks, tops only, chopped
1 large potato, peeled and diced
2 cups boiling water
4 cups milk, scalded
2-3 cups cabbage, finely shredded
1 tsp. salt
$^1/_2$ tsp. pepper
2 tbsp. butter

In a large saucepan, combine the onion, carrots, celery and potato. Pour the boiling water on top, then cover and simmer over medium-low heat for 20 minutes, or until the potato is tender. Mash the vegetables with a fork, but do not worry if some stay whole. Add the scalded milk and bring to a fast rolling boil. Add the cabbage, salt and pepper. Simmer, uncovered for 10-15 minutes. Add the butter. Stir.

To serve: toast 6 slices of bread, butter each well, then place one slice in the bottom of each soup bowl. Sprinkle with grated Parmesan cheese and pour the soup on top. Serves 6.

Mom's Helpers

To make your own pilaf seasoning quickly, combine two pulverized chicken bouillon cubes with $^1/_2$ tsp. each of rosemary, thyme, and marjoram. Mix this with one cup of raw rice and cook in two cups of water in a covered saucepan over low heat. Season with salt if desired.

CREAM OF CORN SOUP

1 onion, chopped fine
1 celery stalk, diced
 $^1/_4$ cup butter or 3 tbsp. bacon fat
4 cups milk
1 (15 oz. can) canned corn (creamed or kernel)
 $^1/_4$ tsp. curry powder
   Salt and pepper to taste

Saute the onion and celery in the butter or bacon fat just until the onion is lightly browned. Add the flour to the onion mixture and blend together thoroughly. Add milk, stir until thickened, then add the corn, curry powder, salt and pepper. Mix well, cover and leave over very low heat until ready to serve. (For a thicker soup, use cream-style corn; for a lighter soup, use corn kernels). Serves 6.

CREAM OF LEEK SOUP

3 large leeks
2 tbsp. lemon juice
3 tbsp. butter
2 tbsp. finely chopped onion
2 tbsp. flour
1 tsp. salt
 $^1/_4$ tsp. black pepper
3 cups chicken stock
2 cups light table cream
   Ground nutmeg
2 tbsp. chopped parsley

Prepare leeks. Wash and cut in thin slices. Put in a medium saucepan, cover with boiling water and add lemon juice. Bring to a boil, reduce heat to medium and boil 5 minutes. Drain leeks, then add butter and onion. Stir over medium heat 5 minutes. Sprinkle in flour, salt and pepper and stir to blend. Remove from heat and stir in chicken stock. Return to high heat and bring to a boil, stirring. Turn heat to low, partially cover and simmer 30 minutes, stirring occasionally.

At serving time, heat cream to scalding over medium heat and stir into soup. Sprinkle lightly with nutmeg and parsley. Serves 4 to 6.

Mom's Helpers
Use oil to saute vegetables for chilled soup — butter solidifies when it is cold.

CREAMED GREEN PEA SOUP

1 chicken bouillon cube
1 cup water
3 cups frozen green peas
1 small onion, diced
1 tbsp. butter
2 tbsp. flour
3 cups whole milk
 Salt and pepper to taste

Add the bouillon cube to the water and bring to a boil. Then add the frozen green peas and boil for 10 minutes or until peas are tender. Make a puree of the peas by using a blender or food processor. Fry the onion lightly in the butter. Add the flour, blend well, then slowly add the milk. Stir until smooth and add the pureed peas. Stir well, add salt and pepper to taste and serve hot. Garnish with chopped fresh or dried mint. Serves 6.

EGG DROP SOUP

1 stewing chicken, cut up
1 sliced carrot
1 stalk sliced celery
1 whole peeled onion
2 crushed cloves of garlic
 Parsley sprigs
1 tsp. pepper
1 tsp. salt
1 tsp. basil
5 cups water
1 cup white wine (optional)

Place all ingredients in a large pot and boil gently for about 1 to 1½ hours. Remove chicken. Strain stock.

1 quart chicken stock
½ cup fresh chopped mushrooms
½ cup cooked chicken, shredded
3 eggs
½ cup chopped green onions and chopped fresh parsley

Bring broth to a boil over medium heat. Add chicken and mushrooms. Beat eggs well, and add to broth a spoonful at a time, stirring after each spoonful. Garnish with green onions and parsley and serve.

MINESTRONE SOUP

   2 tbsp. butter
  $^1/_2$ cup chopped onion
   4 cups beef broth
   2 cups canned tomatoes
   2 cups water
 $1^1/_2$ cups kernel corn
 $1^1/_2$ cups baby lima beans
 $1^1/_2$ cups diced carrots
 $^3/_4$ cup broken pieces of uncooked spaghetti
   2 tsp. salt
 $^1/_2$ tsp. oregano
 $^1/_4$ tsp. pepper

Saute onion in butter until tender. Stir in remaining ingredients and bring to a boil, cover and turn heat to simmer for 20-25 minutes. Serves 8.

ONION SOUP WITH CHEESE

   3 tbsp. butter
   6 medium onions, thinly sliced
   6 beef flavoured bouillon cubes
   6 cups boiling water
     $^1/_2$-inch slices French bread
     Butter
     Grated Parmesan cheese
     Salt and pepper to taste
   2 tbsp. dry sherry (optional)

Melt butter in a large saucepan. Add onions and saute until golden brown. Dissolve the cubes in boiling water. Bring to a boil, reduce heat to simmer, cover, and continue simmering for 40 minutes. Broil one side of bread slices in the oven until golden then butter untoasted side and cover with cheese. Broil until cheese is golden. Season soup and add sherry. Put 1 or 2 broiled bread slices, cheese side up, in each soup bowl and pour in soup. Serves 6.

Mom's Helpers

When you want the flavor in the cooking liquid for making soup, sauce, etc., always start the meat or poultry in cold, cold water to draw out the juices.

If a soup in your soup kettle is too salty, add a potato or two, peeled and quartered. The potato will absorb some of the saltiness — and it is edible, too.

VICHYSSOISE

4 thinly sliced leeks
¹/₄ cup sliced onions
3 tbsp. butter
4 cups chicken stock
5 sliced potatoes
2 cups milk
1 cup cream
Salt, to taste
Pepper
Chopped chives

Very lightly brown leeks and onions in the melted butter. Add stock and potatoes bringing to a boil. Simmer 35 minutes. Strain mixture through a sieve or put through a blender. Add milk to mixture and heat. Add cream, salt, pepper. Stir in well and chill. Serve in glasses or cups. Garnish with chopped chives. (By using a blender, a thicker vichyssoise results.)

Mom's Helpers

Dress up cream of tomato soup by floating a thin slice of orange, or some chopped fresh parsley on the surface of the soup.

Use white pepper in light soups and sauces instead of black pepper — black specks would be most unattractive.

Thicken a long-cooking soup with a handful of oatmeal added at the beginning. The oatmeal adds texture and body and scarcely more calories.

Make a "blender soup" every time you clean out the refrigerator. Use up bits of cooked vegetables, sauces and such; whirl them in a blender to desired consistency. The pureed vegetables will thicken the soup, or if the soup is too thick, more broth or stock will thin it. With compatible leftovers, spiked with a little imagination, you can come up with some delectable hot or cold soups.

APPLE AND GOLDEN RAISIN SLAW

    1 cup white or rose wine
    1 cup golden raisins
    1 tbsp. lemon juice
    2 red apples, cored and diced
    1 yellow apple, cored and diced
    1 head cabbage
    1 cup lemon dressing (recipe follows)

Warm wine; add raisins and set aside to cool. Sprinkle apples with lemon juice then add raisin-wine mixture and chopped cabbage. Toss with lemon dressing and chill before serving. Serves 6.

Lemon dressing:

    $^1/_2$ cup sugar
    2 tsp. dry mustard
    $^2/_3$ cup lemon juice
    $^1/_2$ cup salad oil
    $^2/_3$ cup sour cream

Combine sugar, mustard, and lemon juice in a blender. Slowly add $^1/_2$ cup salad oil. Transfer ingredients to a bowl and stir in $^2/_3$ cup sour cream. Makes about 2 cups. Serve extra dressing on fruit salad; keeps one week refrigerated.

BEAN SALAD

    1 (10 oz.) pkg. frozen cut green beans
    1 (10 oz.) pkg. frozen cut yellow beans
 $1^1/_4$ cups canned drained kidney beans
    1 cup canned drained lima beans
    1 cup garbanzo beans
    1 (10 oz.) can drained and sliced water chestnuts
  $^1/_2$ cup cider vinegar
  $^1/_3$ cup salad oil
  $^1/_3$ cup sugar
  $^1/_2$ tsp. salt
  $^1/_8$ tsp. pepper

Cook green and yellow beans according to package directions; drain. Combine green and yellow beans with the next four ingredients in a large bowl. Stir together vinegar, oil, sugar, salt and pepper. Pour over beans and toss lightly to coat. Cover and refrigerate overnight to blend flavours. Serves 5.

CANTALOUPE SALAD

2 medium-sized ripe cantaloupes
$^1/_2$ cup mayonnaise
$^1/_2$ cup thick sour cream
$^1/_2$ tsp. salt
$^1/_8$ tsp. pepper

Pare and remove the seeds from the cantaloupes. Cut cantaloupes into $^3/_4$-inch cubes, put into a large bowl and set aside. Mix together the next 4 ingredients, blending well. Pour half the dressing onto cantaloupe and toss lightly. Chill cantaloupe and remaining dressing in refrigerator for about 1 hour. Remove from refrigerator and place individual servings on crisp lettuce leaves. Top each serving with the remaining dressing. Serves 8.

CAESAR SALAD

1 clove garlic, halved
$^1/_2$ cup olive oil
8 anchovy fillets, cut up
1 tsp. Worcestershire sauce
$^1/_2$ tsp. salt
$^1/_4$ tsp. dry mustard
$^1/_8$ tsp. pepper
1 large or 2 small bunches romaine lettuce, washed and chilled
1 coddled egg
1 lemon
$^1/_2$ cup grated Parmesan cheese
   Garlic croutons

Just before serving, rub large salad bowl with cut clove of garlic. Add oil, anchovies, Worcestershire sauce, salt, mustard, and pepper; mix thoroughly. Into salad bowl, tear romaine into bite-size pieces (about 12 cups). Toss until leaves glisten. Break egg onto romaine, squeeze juice from lemon over romaine. Toss until leaves are well coated. Sprinkle croutons and cheese over salad and toss. Serves 6.

Garlic Croutons:

Heat oven to 400 degrees F. Trim crusts from 4 slices white bread. Generously butter both sides of bread slices, sprinkle with $^1/_4$ tsp. garlic powder. Cut into $^1/_2$-inch cubes, place in baking pan. Bake 10 to 15 minutes, stirring occasionally, until golden brown and crisp.

Coddled Egg:

Place cold egg with shell on in warm water in a small saucepan (this prevents shell from breaking). In another saucepan heat to boiling point enough water to completely cover the egg. With a spoon, immerse egg into the boiling water. Remove pan from heat, cover and let stand 30 seconds. Immediately cool egg in cold water.

BANANA ORANGE SALAD DRESSING

1 medium banana
2 tbsp. frozen orange juice concentrate
2 tsp. honey
1 cup orange flavoured yogurt

In a blender, combine cut up banana, frozen orange juice, and honey. Cover and blend at medium speed until smooth. Fold in yogurt. Cover and refrigerate several hours. Serve as fruit dressing or fruit dip. Yields 1½ cups.

CUCUMBER DRESSING

$^1/_3$ cup mayonnaise
$^1/_2$ tsp. salt
1 tsp. fresh dill, chopped
$^1/_4$ tsp. pepper
$^1/_3$ cup lemon juice
1 cup buttermilk
1 pared, diced, drained cucumber

Put all ingredients except cucumber into blender and blend until smooth. Add cucumber and chill.

CURRIED CHICKEN SALAD

1 cup plain yogurt
$^1/_3$ cup mayonnaise or salad dressing
2 tbsp. sweet relish
$^1/_2$ tsp. salt (to taste)
1 tsp. curry powder
4 cups cubed cooked chicken
1 cup sliced celery
$^3/_4$ cup sliced radishes
$^1/_4$ cup chopped green onion

Combine the first five ingredients, stir well, cover and refrigerate at least one hour to blend flavours. Mix the last four ingredients in a large bowl. Add the refrigerated mixture and toss lightly to coat. Serves 6.

Mom's Helpers
To keep green salads fresh for a longer time, sprinkle the greens with the juice of a lemon or lime.

EGG SALAD

4 slices dry bread
2 cloves garlic
4 hard-boiled eggs
1 head lettuce
1 cup French dressing

Remove crusts from 1-inch thick bread slices; rub both sides with garlic. Cut bread into small pieces. Chop hard-boiled eggs. Shred lettuce into salad bowl. Add bread pieces and chopped eggs; toss together lightly. Add French dressing to moisten. Toss. Yields 6.

GINGER LIME DRESSING

$^1/_4$ cup honey
$^1/_4$ cup light rum or orange juice
2 tbsp. lime juice
1 tbsp. chopped crystallized ginger
1 tsp. grated lime peel

Combine all ingredients and shake well before using. Serve with fresh fruits and yogurt.

GOLDEN RICE SALAD

$^1/_4$ cup salad oil
2 tbsp. vinegar
2 tbsp. prepared mustard
$1^1/_2$ tsp. salt
$^1/_8$ tsp. pepper
$1^1/_2$ cups uncooked rice
$3^1/_2$ cups chicken broth
1 cup ripe olives, cut in large pieces
2 hard cooked eggs, diced
$^1/_4$ cup dill pickles, chopped
$^1/_4$ cup pimiento
1 small onion, minced
$^1/_2$ cup mayonnaise

Boil the rice in the chicken broth — it yields $4^1/_2$ cups cooked rice. Blend together salad oil, vinegar, mustard, salt, and pepper; pour over hot cooked rice. Toss and set aside to cool. When cooled, add remaining ingredients and toss. Chill thoroughly. Serve on lettuce leaf and garnish with extra sliced eggs. Serves 8 one-cup servings. The mixture can be molded individually by spooning into 1-cup molds before chilling.

SAVORY MOUSSE SALAD

1 cup tomato sauce
8 oz. pkg. cream cheese, cut in chunks
1 envelope unflavoured gelatin
$1/4$ cup cold water
$1/2$ cup diced celery
$1/2$ cup diced green pepper
1 cup cooked ham, finely chopped
2 green onions, finely chopped
$1/2$ tsp. Worcestershire sauce
Pinch of black pepper

Combine tomato sauce and cream cheese in top of double boiler. Heat and whisk until smooth. Meanwhile, soften gelatin in cold water for 5 minutes. Stir in tomato-cheese mixture and continue heating until gelatin is dissolved. Chill until mixture starts to set. Stir in remaining ingredients. Spoon into a 4-cup mold and chill until set. Unmold on a bed of lettuce. Serves 5.

SPRING DAIRY SALAD

$1^1/2$ envelopes gelatin
3 tbsp. cold water
1 cup cottage cheese sieved
1 cup cheddar cheese, grated
$1/2$ tsp. salt
$1/8$ tsp. white pepper
2 tbsp. chopped pimento
2 tbsp. chopped green pepper
$1/2$ cup diced cheddar cheese
2 cups whipping cream

Soak gelatin in cold water until soft then dissolve by placing over hot water (double boiler). Soften cottage cheese with a little plain cream and press through sieve. Add grated cheese, gelatin, seasoning, pimento, pepper, and diced cheese. Reserve some of the diced cheese to sprinkle in the bottom of the mold. Fold in stiffly beaten cream, turn mixture into wet mold and chill. Serve on a large plate and garnish with fresh strawberries, sliced kiwi fruit, grapes and lettuce.

Mom's Helpers

When making a lettuce salad, break up leaves with fingers. Do not use knives to cut the leaves as this causes discoloration and tarnishing.

SUNFLOWER SALAD

3 large oranges
Lettuce leaves
1/2 cup grated sharp cheese
Pitted olives
Sweet salad dressing

Peel and section oranges. Place lettuce leaves on plates and arrange orange sections to form petals of sunflowers. Put 2 tbsp. of grated cheese in center of each salad. Garnish centers with olives. Serve with dressing of your choice. Serves 4.

TUNA APPLE SALAD

1 cup chunky light tuna
4 medium unpeeled red apples, diced
1 tbsp. lemon juice
1 cup celery, diced
1/2 cup walnuts, chopped
1/2 cup mayonnaise

Sprinkle lemon juice over apples. Combine apples, tuna, celery and walnuts. Toss with mayonnaise. Serve in crisp lettuce cups. Serves 4.

TUNA MACARONI SALAD

1 lb. macaroni
2 cans (7 oz.) solid light tuna
1 1/2 cups finely sliced celery
1 1/4 cups mayonnaise
1/4 cup lemon juice
1/2 cup milk
1/2 tsp. seasoned salt
1/2 tsp. pepper
1/2 cup chopped pimento
Salad greens, tomatoes, or radishes (optional)

Cook macaroni according to package directions. Drain and set aside to cool. Add tuna, celery, mayonnaise, lemon juice, milk, and seasoning. Fold in pimento and chill until serving time. To serve garnish with salad green of your choice. Serves 8.

L. to R.: Savory Cheese Bread Page 63, Molasses Brown Bread, Page 62, Quick Cheese Onion Bread, Page 61, Old Fashioned Bran Muffins, Page 61

QUICK BREADS,
LOAVES,
and
MUFFINS

ANISE BUTTER CRESCENTS

 1/2 cup butter
1 1/2 tsp. crushed aniseed
1 1/2 tsp. finely grated lemon rind
  1 tsp. vanilla
1 1/4 cup sugar
  2 cups sifted all purpose flour

Combine butter, aniseed, lemon rind, and vanilla in a bowl. Beat until creamy, gradually add sugar beating all the time. Stir in flour. Cover bowl and chill dough until it is firm enough to handle. Pinch off a small piece, the size of a small walnut, roll between palms of hands into a rope approx. 2 1/2 inches long. Shape into a crescent and place on ungreased baking sheet. Repeat process, placing them 1 1/2 to 2 inches apart. Bake in 300 degree F. slow oven for 12 minutes or until lightly browned. Let cool 3 to 5 minutes, then transfer from pan. Makes 6 1/2 dozen cookies. (To crush aniseed, place some seeds between 2 sheets of waxed paper and run a rolling pin over them several times . . . they will not crush finely. Measure 1 1/2 teaspoon crushed aniseed).

APPLE PANCAKES

  2 tbsp. butter
10-15 thin, peeled apple slices
  3 eggs, separated
 1/2 cup milk
 1/2 cup pancake mix
  3 tbsp. icing sugar
     Juice and grated peel of 1 lemon
 1/3 cup honey

Melt the butter in a heavy cast iron frying pan. Add the apple slices, cook over medium heat until lightly browned on all sides. Beat the egg whites until stiff and the yolks until creamy. Combine the yolks with the milk, then beat in the pancake mix, stirring until fairly smooth. Fold in egg whites and pour mixture over apples. Cook over medium heat, without stirring, for about three minutes, until golden brown on the underside. Place pan in a 425 degree F. oven and cook about 5 minutes. Remove to a hot platter and sprinkle top with the icing sugar. Heat the lemon juice, peel, and honey together and pour over pancake. Cut the pancake into wedges. Serves 4.

Mom's Helpers
Pancakes or waffles brown more easily if a bit of sugar is added to the batter.

56

APRICOT-DATE-NUT BREAD

$^1/_2$ cup diced apricots
3 cups all-purpose flour (make 1 cup whole-wheat if desired)
3 tsp. baking powder
$^1/_4$ tsp. baking soda
1 tsp. salt
1 cup brown sugar
$^1/_2$ cup chopped dates
1 cup chopped walnuts
1 cup milk
1 egg, well beaten
$^1/_2$ cup maple syrup
$^1/_4$ tsp. maple flavouring

Cover diced apricots with boiling water and let stand 15 minutes. Drain and set aside. Sift together flour, baking powder, baking soda and salt. Mix in brown sugar and dates, apricots and nuts. Mix into another bowl milk, beaten egg, maple syrup, and maple flavouring. Add to flour mixture and beat well. Pour into a well-greased loaf pan. Bake at 350 degrees F. for about $1^1/_4$ hours, or until a toothpick inserted into the centre comes out clean. Cool. Spread with cream cheese and decorate with nuts.

BRAN MOLASSES MUFFINS

1 cup sifted all-purpose flour
2 tbsp. sugar
2 tsp. baking powder
$^1/_4$ tsp. baking soda
$^1/_2$ tsp. salt
$^1/_3$ cup butter
$^3/_4$ cup milk
$^1/_4$ cup molasses
2 eggs, well beaten
$1^1/_4$ cups bran flakes

Sift flour with sugar, baking powder, soda and salt. Cut in butter. Combine milk, molasses and eggs; add to flour mixture. Mix only enough to dampen flour. Fold in cereal. Fill greased muffin pans about two-thirds full. Bake at 400 degrees F. about 20 minutes. Makes 8 to 10 muffins.

Mom's Helpers

Remove a stubborn cake or bread from its tin by wrapping the whole thing in a towel as it comes from the oven and letting it stand for a few minutes. The heat of the just-baked cake or bread will condense and the moisture will loosen it.

BUTTERMILK FLAPJACKS

   1 cup sifted all-purpose flour
   3 tsp. baking powder
 1/4 tsp. salt
   1 tbsp. sugar
   3 eggs
 1/2 cup buttermilk
   2 tbsp. butter, melted

Combine flour, baking powder, salt and sugar and stir lightly with a fork. In a separate bowl, beat eggs until they are light and fluffy, about 2 minutes at high speed on an electric mixer. Add flour mixture and beat until smooth. Add buttermilk and butter and stir only long enough to blend ingredients; do not overbeat. Meanwhile slowly heat griddle or heavy skillet. Test griddle by dropping a few drops of cold water on it. If they sputter, griddle temperature is correct. For each flapjack, drop 1/4 cup batter onto hot griddle. Cook until bubbles form on surface and the edges become dry. Then turn and cook about 2 minutes longer or until nicely browned on underside. Serve with maple syrup and sausages or bacon. Makes 8 medium sized flapjacks.

CARAWAY SEED LOAF

  1/2 cup butter
    1 cup sugar
    2 well beaten eggs
 1 3/4 cups sifted flour
  1/4 tsp. salt
 1 1/2 tsp. baking powder
    1 tsp. nutmeg
    3 tbsp. caraway seed
  1/2 cup milk

Grease a 9 x 5 inch loaf pan. In a large bowl, cream butter and beat in sugar and eggs. In another bowl stir together flour, salt, baking powder, nutmeg and caraway seed. Add dry ingredients to creamed mixture alternately with milk. Stir just enough to blend completely. Pour mixture into prepared pan. Bake at 350 degrees F. for about one hour.

Mom's Helpers

French bread spread with garlic butter can be wrapped up in foil and frozen for future use. Heat in foil in the oven when ready to use.

CARROT LOAF

3 cups flour
2 tsp. soda
2 tsp. baking powder
2 tsp. cinnamon
$^3/_4$ tsp. salt
$1^1/_2$ cup salad oil
4 eggs
2 cups sugar

Beat eggs and sugar well, then beat in oil. Add dry ingredients, then stir in:

3 cups finely grated carrots
1 cup chopped glazed cherries
1 cup chopped dates
1 cup raisins
$1^1/_2$ cup chopped nuts

Pour into 2 greased and lined with wax paper loaf pans. Bake at 350 degrees F for about $1^1/_2$ hours.

CHOCOLATE CHIP MUFFINS

1 cup chocolate chips
1 tbsp. instant coffee
$^1/_4$ cup butter
$1^1/_4$ cup milk
2 eggs
$2^1/_2$ cups all-purpose flour
$^1/_3$ cup sugar
1 tbsp. baking powder
$^1/_2$ tsp. salt

Melt $^1/_2$ cup chocolate chips over low heat, add instant coffee, butter and milk, stirring until well blended. Cool. Beat in egg. Combine flour, sugar, baking powder and salt in large bowl. Add chocolate mixture to dry ingredients, stirring until just moistened. Stir in remaining $^1/_2$ cup chocolate chips. Spoon into large greased muffin tins. Bake at 400 degrees F. for about 20 minutes, until done. Makes 12 large muffins.

Mom's Helpers

A package of granular yeast always indicates its expiry date. Always remember to consult the package for that information before you start mixing your dough.

COTTAGE CHEESE ROLLS

$2/3$ cup finely chopped walnuts
$2/3$ cup well packed brown sugar
3 tbsp. melted butter
1 tsp. vanilla
$1/4$ cup plus 2 tsp. granulated sugar
$1/2$ cup lukewarm water
2 envelopes active dry yeast
3 cups sifted all-purpose flour
$1/2$ tsp. salt
1 cup creamed cottage cheese
$1/2$ cup butter
1 egg

To make filling, combine walnuts, brown sugar, melted butter and vanilla in bowl. Blend ingredients thoroughly; set aside. Dissolve 2 tsp. granulated sugar in lukewarm water. Sprinkle yeast over water and let stand 10 minutes. In separate bowl combine flour, salt, remaining $1/4$ cup of granulated sugar and cottage cheese in a large bowl. Using a pastry blender, cut in butter until mixture has consistency of coarse corn meal. Stir yeast. Add egg to stirred yeast and blend well. Add yeast mixture to dry ingredients and mix thoroughly. Turn onto floured board. The dough will be sticky. Turn and knead it 2 or 3 times to coat with flour. Roll out dough into 12-inch square. Spread walnut filling evenly over dough. Roll up as a jelly roll. Pinch dough together firmly on edges. With the sealed side down and using a very sharp knife, cut roll crosswise into 18 even slices. Arrange 9 slices, cut side up, in greased 9-inch square cake pan. Repeat with remaining 9 slices. Cover pans with a clean towel and let dough rise in a warm place, for about 1 hour or until double in bulk. Bake in 375 degrees F. for 15 to 20 minutes or until rolls are nicely browned. Unmold onto a wire rack and allow to cool. Sprinkle with icing sugar. Makes 18 rolls.

Mom's Helpers

To intensify the sweetness of any dish, add a pinch of salt.

For yeast breads, best results are obtained by softening the yeast in warm water which contains a small amount of sugar to start the action of the yeast. No shortening should be added to the dough until about one half of the flour has been worked in. Fat seems to coat the yeast cells with a film that the tiny plants have difficulty penetrating when fermenting, thus causing slow rising dough.

OLD FASHIONED BRAN MUFFINS

1 cup boiling water
3 cups bran cereal
$^1/_2$ cup margarine
1 cup raisins
$^1/_2$ cup nut meats
2 eggs
2 cups buttermilk
$^1/_2$ cup molasses
2 cups all-purpose flour
$^1/_2$ cup sugar
2 tsp. baking powder
1 tsp. baking soda
$^3/_4$ tsp. salt

Pour the boiling water over the cereal, margarine and raisins in a bowl. Stir and cool. Add eggs, buttermilk, molasses, and nuts; stir until well blended. Mix dry ingredients in a large bowl. Add cereal mixture to dry ingredients and stir until just moistened. Pour into greased muffin tins or paper baking cups placed inside muffin tins, $^1/_4$ inch from the top. Bake at 400 degrees F. for about 20 minutes. Makes 24 large muffins. This batter will keep in the refrigerator up to 4 weeks.

QUICK CHEESE ONION BREAD

$^1/_2$ cup onions, chopped and browned
2 cups all purpose flour
3 tsp. baking powder
$^1/_4$ tsp. salt
1 egg
1 tbsp. shortening
1 cup milk
1 cup mild cheese, grated
1 tbsp. poppy seed
2 tbsp. butter
$^1/_4$ cup shortening

Sift together flour, baking powder and salt. Combine egg, milk and melted shortening and add to dry ingredients stirring just to blend. Add cooked onion and $^1/_2$ cup grated cheese. Spread in 8-inch deep round baking dish. Sprinkle remaining $^1/_2$ cup grated cheese and poppy seed on top. Drizzle with melted butter. Bake in 400 degree F. oven for 25 minutes. Cut in pie-shaped pieces. Serves 8.

FIG LOAF

$^3/_4$ cup brown sugar
2 tbsp. soft shortening
1 egg
$1^1/_2$ cups milk
3 cups sifted all-purpose flour
$3^1/_2$ tsp. baking powder
$^3/_4$ tsp. salt
$^1/_2$ tsp. mace
$^3/_4$ cup chopped nuts
1 cup ground figs

Measure out sugar, shortening and egg into a bowl. Blend. Stir in milk. Sift flour, baking powder, salt, and mace together, then add into the first mixture and stir well. Add nuts and figs and blend well. Spoon into a greased 9 x 5 x 3 inch loaf pan and spread evenly. Let stand for 20 minutes. Bake about 1 hour and 10 minutes at 350 degrees F. A toothpick inserted into the center should come out clean when loaf is done.

MOLASSES BROWN BREAD

1 cup all-purpose flour
1 tsp. baking soda
$^1/_2$ tsp. salt
$^1/_2$ tsp. cinnamon
1 egg
1 cup wheat bran cereal
$^1/_2$ cup seedless raisins
2 tbsp. butter
$^1/_3$ cup molasses
$^3/_4$ cup very hot water

Blend together flour, soda, salt and cinnamon; set aside. In large mixing bowl, beat egg until foamy. Add cereal, raisins, butter and molasses; blend. Add water and stir until butter is melted. Add dry ingredients, mixing only until combined. Fill 2 greased metal cans, $4^1/_4$ inches deep and 3 inches across, about $^2/_3$ full or spread batter evenly in one greased 9 x 5 x 3-inch loaf pan. Bake at 350 degrees F. for about 45 minutes for bread in cans or about 35 minutes for loaf bread. Bread is done when wooden pick inserted near the center comes out clean. Remove from cans or pans; let cool slightly. Slice and serve warm. Makes 2 small or 1 large loaf.

Mom's Helpers

To facilitate turning a large pancake, hold a large, lightly greased pot cover in your hand; invert the pancake onto it and slide the pancake into the skillet to fry the second side.

ROLLED TEA BISCUITS

    2 cups all-purpose flour
    3 tsp. baking powder
  $^1/_2$ tsp. salt
  $^1/_3$ cup butter
    1 cup milk

Measure flour, baking powder, and salt. Stir thoroughly to blend. Cut in butter, using pastry blender. Make a hollow in center and add milk, stirring lightly with fork. Mix only until soft dough is formed. Turn onto a lightly floured board and knead gently for 15 seconds. Roll out gently with a rolling pin to $^1/_2$ inch thickness. Cut with a cookie cutter, making one sharp cut for each. Place on ungreased baking sheet, 1-inch apart. Bake in hot oven 450 degrees F. for 12 to 15 minutes. Yields 12 biscuits.

DROP BISCUITS — Use $^1/_4$ cup more milk and drop from a spoon onto greased baking sheet.

TOPPING FOR FRUIT COBBLERS — Add 1 tbsp. sugar and 1 additional tbsp. butter to half the drop biscuit recipe.

SAVORY CHEDDAR BREAD

    2 cups all-purpose flour
    4 tsp. baking powder
    1 tbsp. sugar
  $^1/_2$ tsp. onion salt
  $^1/_2$ tsp. crushed oregano
  $^1/_4$ tsp. dry mustard
  $1^1/_4$ cups shredded cheddar cheese
    1 egg, well beaten
    1 cup milk
    1 tbsp. butter, melted

Stir together in a bowl flour, baking powder, sugar, onion, salt, oregano, dry mustard and cheese. Combine egg, milk and butter; add all at once to dry ingredients, stirring just until moistened. Spread batter in a greased $4^1/_2 \times 8^1/_2 \times 2^1/_2$ inch loaf pan. Bake in a preheated 350 degree F. oven 45 minutes. Cool 10 minutes on wire rack. Remove from pan. Slice to serve.

Mom's Helpers

Allow more time to bake two sheets of cookies in the same oven than one sheet. There is an extra pan and dough that have to reach the prescribed temperature before the cookies start to bake. This holds equally true for multiple batches of cakes, pies, or muffins.

SOUR CREAM SCONES

$1^3/_4$ cups sifted all-purpose flour
  2 tsp. baking powder
 $^3/_4$ tsp. soda
 $^1/_2$ tsp. salt
 $^1/_4$ cup sugar
  1 tsp. each orange and lemon rind
 $^1/_4$ cup currants
  2 tbsp. butter
  1 egg beaten
 $^2/_3$ to $^3/_4$ cup sour cream

Sift dry ingredients, add orange and lemon rind and currants. Cut in butter, add egg together with sufficient sour cream to make a soft dough. Turn onto a lightly floured board and knead gently until smooth. Pat or roll into a circle about $^3/_4$ inch thickness. With a knife mark into six sections like the spokes in a wheel. Place on a greased baking sheet and brush with cream or egg yolk diluted with 2 tablespoons milk. Sprinkle with granulated sugar. Bake at 400 degrees F. for about 15 minutes. Serve warm, split and buttered.

Mom's Helpers

To prevent water from running down your arms when washing walls and ceiling, wrap a wash cloth around your wrist and secure it with a rubber band.

Add wine to flavour slow-cooking stews and ragouts. The alcohol in the wine boils away, but the flavour of the wine remains. The acid in the wine also serves as a tenderizer for the meat.

For most tender crepes, let the crepe batter stand for an hour or two before it is used. The flour in the batter keeps absorbing the liquid like a sponge and you may find that you will have to add a little more liquid after the resting period to thin it out. The crepe batter should be the consistency of heavy cream.

CAKES,
COOKIES,
and
SQUARES

APRICOT NUT BARS

$^2/_3$ cup dried apricots, packed
$1^1/_2$ cups water
$^1/_3$ cup soft butter
$^1/_4$ cup sugar
  1 cup sifted all-purpose flour
  1 cup brown sugar, packed
  2 eggs
$^1/_3$ cup sifted all-purpose flour
$^1/_2$ tsp. baking powder
$^1/_4$ tsp. salt
  1 tsp. vanilla
$^1/_2$ cup chopped walnuts
   Icing sugar

Grease an 8-inch square pan. Combine apricots and water in a small sauce-pan. Bring to a boil, turn down heat, cover and simmer 10 minutes. Drain, cook, and chop finely.

Combine butter, $^1/_4$ cup sugar and 1 cup flour in a bowl, working with fingers until mixture is crumbly. Press firmly into the pan. Bake 25 minutes or until lightly browned. Remove from the oven. Beat brown sugar and eggs together until very creamy, add in the $^1/_3$ cup flour, baking powder, and salt. Stir in vanilla, walnuts and chopped apricots. Spread on top of first layer in the pan. Return to the oven and bake about 30 minutes more or until top is set. Set pan on cake rack and allow to cool to lukewarm. Sift icing sugar generously over the top. Cool completely and cut into bars.

Mom's Helpers

Be sure to use a large saucepan for cooking jam to allow for expansion during a full rolling boil. The pan should only be half full because a full rolling boil cannot be stirred down.

Make lower-calorie whipped cream by substituting stiffly-beaten egg whites for part of the cream. Fold the beaten egg white into the whipped cream shortly before using. The mixture does not have the holding power of all cream, but it is as delicious and looks almost the same.

APRICOT SLICE

1 cup dried apricots, packed
Cold water
1 cup flour
$^1/_2$ tsp. baking powder
$^1/_4$ tsp. salt
$^1/_4$ cup brown sugar
$^1/_2$ cup butter
2 eggs
1 cup brown sugar
$^1/_2$ cup all purpose flour
$^1/_2$ tsp. vanilla
$^1/_2$ cup chopped nuts
Icing sugar

Cover apricots with cold water in small saucepan. Bring to a boil, turn down heat and boil gently 10 minutes. Drain and lay on paper towelling to cool and dry, then cut into small pieces. Grease an 8-inch squre pan. Sift 1 cup flour, baking powder and salt into a bowl. Add $^1/_4$ cup brown sugar and blend with a fork. Add butter and mix and blend until mixture looks like shortbread. Press into prepared pan. Bake 10 minutes. Beat eggs lightly with a fork. Add 1 cup brown sugar, $^1/_2$ cup flour, vanilla, nuts and apricots, mix well. Spread on top of dough in pan. Return to oven and bake 30 minutes or until set. Cut into bars while warm. Roll in icing sugar before storing.

APRICOT TREAT

$1^1/_2$ cups apricot nectar
$1^1/_2$ cups raisins
$^1/_3$ cup dried apricots (about 12) cut fine

Mix together and simmer for five minutes. Add 1 tbsp. grated orange rind. Set aside.

$2^3/_4$ cups sifted flour
2 tsp. soda
$^1/_2$ tsp. salt
$^1/_2$ cup chopped walnuts
1 tbsp. butter
1 cup sugar
1 unbeaten egg
$^1/_3$ cup cream

Cream together, butter, sugar, egg and cream. In another bowl mix flour, soda, salt and walnuts together. Blend dry ingredients alternately with fruit mixture into the creamed butter mixture, stirring well. Turn into two well-greased and lightly floured 8 x 4 x $2^1/_2$ inch loaf pan. Bake in 350 degrees F. for 50 to 60 minutes. Cool thoroughly before slicing.

BUTTER SHORTBREAD

 1 cup soft butter
$^1/_2$ cup brown sugar, packed
 1 tsp. vanilla
 2 to $2^1/_4$ cups sifted all-purpose flour

Heat oven to 325 degrees F. Beat butter until fluffy. Add sugar and vanilla slowly, beating continually. Add flour gradually, kneading the last portion into dough by hand until mixture "cracks". Roll out dough on lightly floured board to $^1/_4$-inch thickness. Cut into desired shapes, decorated with pieces of cherries is desired. Place on ungreased baking sheets and bake at 325 degrees F. for about 20 minutes. Makes 2 dozen.

CARAWAY COOKIES

 3 cups sifted all-purpose flour
$^1/_2$ tsp. salt
$^1/_2$ tsp. soda
$1^1/_2$ tsp. baking powder
$^1/_2$ cup butter
$^2/_3$ cup brown sugar, packed
 2 tsp. caraway seeds
 2 eggs
 1 cup sour cream
$1^1/_2$ tsp. vanilla
   Sugar

Sift flour, salt, soda and baking powder together into a bowl. Add butter and cut in finely. Add sugar and caraway seeds and blend well with a fork. (Place seeds into a plastic bag and roll them with a rolling pin to crush them slightly). Beat egg, cream and vanilla together with a fork and stir in. Chill dough thoroughly. Heat oven to 350 degrees F. Roll dough $^1/_8$ inch thick and cut with a 2-inch cookie cutter. Place on greased cookie sheet, sprinkle with sugar, and bake 12 to 15 minutes, until lightly browned. Makes $5^1/_2$ dozen.

Mom's Helpers

Try adding honey to whipped cream in place of sugar. A teaspoon of honey adds a sweet, delicious flavour, and the whipped cream stays firm longer.

CHEWY GINGER COOKIES

$1/2$ cup brown sugar
1 cup soft butter
1 cup molasses
$2/3$ cup cold water
$4^1/2$ cups flour
3 tsp. soda
2 tsp. ginger
$1/2$ tsp. cloves
$1/2$ tsp. cinnamon
$1/2$ tsp. salt
Granulated sugar

Cream brown sugar and butter. Stir in molasses and water. Sift flour, soda, ginger, cloves, cinnamon and salt together into mixture and blend well. Chill dough at least 4 hours. Heat oven to 400 degrees F. Roll dough into a square $1/8$ inch thick and cut into 2-inch squares. Put on ungreased cookie sheet and sprinkle generously with granulated sugar. Bake about 7 minute or until tops spring back when lightly touched. Yields approx. 6 dozen.

CHOCOLATE COOKIES

$1/2$ cup soft butter
$1^1/2$ cups sugar
2 eggs
2 oz. unsweetened melted chocolate
$2^3/4$ cups sifted flour
$1/2$ tsp. soda
1 cup evaporated milk
1 tsp. vanilla
1 cup chopped nuts

Combine butter, sugar, eggs and chocolate in bowl and beat until mixture is fluffy. Sift together flour, soda, and salt. Combine milk and vanilla. Add dry ingredients to creamed mixture alternately with milk, stirring well. Stir in nuts. Drop by teaspoonful on lightly greased cookie sheet. Bake 10 to 12 minutes at 375 degrees F. Blend the following ingredients together and ice:

3 tbps. soft butter
$1^1/2$ cups sifted icing sugar
1 oz. unsweetened melted chocolate
2 tbsp. cream
$1/2$ tsp. vanilla.

CRISPIE COOKIES

1 cup sugar
1 heaping tsp. brown sugar
1 tsp. vanilla
1 cup butter
1 egg
Dash of salt
1 tsp. soda
1 tsp. cream of tartar
1¹/₂ cups flour
2 cups rice krispies

Mix ingredients in the order given. Roll in balls the size of a walnut, then press with a fork. Bake at 350 degrees F. oven 12 to 15 minutes.

DREAM CAKE BARS

³/₄ cup melted butter
¹/₄ cup brown sugar
1¹/₂ cups flour

Cut through with pastry blender and press into a 9-inch cake pan. Bake at 300 degrees F. until brown. Mix the following:

1¹/₂ cups brown sugar
1 cup chopped walnuts
1 cup coconut flakes
³/₄ cup chopped dates
3 tbsp. flour
¹/₄ tsp. baking powder
2 eggs, beaten
Dash of salt
Very small bottle maraschino cherries

Spread this mixture over the baked mixture. Dot with maraschino cherries and bake at 300 degrees F. for 30 minutes. Cut into bars.

Mom's Helpers

When necessary to cover a bad stain or patch on a child's bedspread, cut press-on patches in animal shapes. Children love it.

Frost cupcakes in half the time. Dip the top of each cupcake into soft frosting, twirl slightly, then quickly turn right side up.

Rum Balls, Page 76, Rich Dark Fruit Cake, Page 85
Rubies and Emeralds, Page 78

FRYPAN COOKIES

1 cup sugar
2 eggs well beaten
1/2 lb. dates
1 tsp. vanilla
Pinch of salt
3 cups rice krispies
Fine shredded coconut

Combine all the ingredients in a frypan. Cook slowly stirring constantly 10-15 minutes until thickened. Cool. Stir in 3 cups Rice Krispies. Shape into balls and roll in coconut.

HONEY COOKIES

1 cup liquid honey
1/3 cup soft butter
2 eggs
2 cups sifted all-purpose flour
2 tsp. baking powder
1/2 tsp. salt
1 tsp. cinnamon
1/4 tsp. cloves
1/4 tsp. soda
3 cups rolled oats
1 cup finely grated carrots
1 cup seedless raisins
1 cup chopped walnuts

Combine first three ingredients and beat well. Sift flour, baking powder, salt, cinnamon, cloves and soda together. Add to creamed mixture. Add rolled oats, carrots, raisins and walnuts and blend well. Drop by teaspoonful onto cookie sheet. Flatten with fork. Bake 12 to 15 minutes at 375 degrees F. Makes approx. 6 dozen. Store in an air tight container.

Mom's Helpers

Bring out the sweetness of corn by adding a tablespoon of corn syrup to the water in which the corn is being cooked.

When preparing a cake batter that calls for the alternate addition of flour and liquid, start and finish with the flour. Your cake will be lighter as a result.

LIGHT CAKE BROWNIES
(one-step mix)

$^1/_3$ cup vegetable oil
2 squares (2 oz.) unsweetened chocolate
1 cup water
$^1/_2$ cup sugar
2 eggs
$1^3/_8$ cup all-purpose flour
$^1/_2$ tsp. salt
$^1/_2$ tsp. baking soda
$^1/_4$ tsp. baking powder
$^1/_2$ tsp. vanilla
1 (6 oz.) pkg semi-sweet chocolate chips
$^1/_2$ cup chopped wanuts

Heat oil and chocolate in an 8-inch square cake pan, in the oven, 350 degrees F. for about 4 minutes. Add water, sugar, eggs, flour, salt, baking soda, baking powder, and vanilla. Beat with a fork until smooth, about 2 minutes. Spread evenly in the pan. Sprinkle with chocolate chips and nuts. Bake at 350 degrees F. for 40 minutes or until a toothpick comes out clean. Serves 8.

MMM-BUTTER BARS

1 cup butter
$^1/_2$ cup sugar
$^3/_4$ cup cocoa
2 eggs, beaten
2 tsp. vanilla
4 cups crushed wafer crumbs
2 cups fine coconut
1 cup finely chopped walnuts

Melt the butter in medium sized saucepan and add sugar, cocoa and beaten eggs. Cook, stirring constantly, until it thickens. Add the wafer crumbs, coconut and walnuts. Mix well. Grease two 8-inch square pans and press mixture firmly into the pan. Set aside.

$^1/_2$ cup butter
6 tbsp. milk
4 tbsp. vanilla custard powder
4 cups icing sugar
8 oz. semi-sweet chocolate
2 tbsp. butter

Cream butter until fluffy. Mix milk and custard powder together and add to the butter. Blend in icing sugar until the mixture is smooth. Spread evenly over the cooled base. Chill in the refrigerator for about 20 minutes. Melt the chocolate and butter in a small pot and then spread over the custard icing. Chill for $^1/_2$ hour in refrigerator. Cut into 48 bars.

OATMEAL REFRIGERATOR SHORTBREAD

1 cup soft butter
1 cup sifted icing sugar
2 tsp. vanilla
2 cups sifted all-purpose flour
1 cup quick cooking rolled oats
   Chocolate decorating candies (optional)

Cream butter until fluffy. Beat in sugar and vanilla. Blend in flour, then rolled oats. Mix with hands until very well blended. Divide dough into two equal parts and shape each into a roll 1½ inches in diameter. Roll each part in chocolate decorating candies to coat outside (press in with hands to make them stick well). Wrap in waxed paper and chill for 8 hours. Heat oven to 350 degrees F. Cut cookie rolls into ¼-inch thickness, place on ungreased cookie sheet and bake 10 to 12 minutes or until lightly browned. Makes 3½ dozen.

PEANUT BUTTER SQUARES

½ cup brown sugar
½ cup corn syrup
1 cup crunchy style peanut butter
5 cups rice krispies
½ cup chopped salted nuts
   Butter icing (recipe follows)

Combine sugar, corn syrup, and peanut butter in top of double boiler. Set over hot water and heat until smooth and blended. Remove from heat. Add rice krispies and peanuts and blend well. Pack mixture firmly into a 9-inch square pan. Cool and ice with a thin layer of Butter Icing. Cut into squares.

Butter Icing:

1½ tbsp. butter
1 cup sifted icing sugar
1 tbsp. cream
½ tsp. vanilla

Blend all ingredients, adding enough cream to make mixture smooth and easy to spread.

Mom's Helpers

If fruit does not yield as much prepared fruit as needed in a recipe, up to ½ cup of water may be added.

PINEAPPLE FILLED COOKIES

2/3 cup butter
1 cup sugar
2 eggs
2 1/2 cups flour
1/4 tsp. soda
1/4 tsp. salt
2 tbsp. thick sour cream
1 tsp. vanilla

Cream butter, add sugar and beat until light. Add well beaten eggs. Sift flour, soda and salt together and alternately add cream. Stir in vanilla.
Roll thin, cut in 3-inch rounds and place a teaspoon of filling on each (recipe follows). Fold over like a turnover, pressing edges gently together. Bake at 425 degrees F. for 10 minutes. Remove from pan and cool on racks.

PINEAPPLE FILLING

2/3 cup sugar
3 tbsp. flour
1 cup crushed pineapple, drained well
3 tbsp. lemon juice
2 tbsp. butter
1/2 cup pineapple juice

Blend sugar and flour. Add the remaining ingredients. Cook slowly, stirring constantly until filling thickens. Cool and fill cookies.

QUICK SHORTBREAD

1 cup butter
1/2 cup sifted icing sugar
2 1/2 cups sifted flour
Red or green sprinkles for trim

Heat oven to 450 degrees F. Beat butter until light and gradually add sugar, beating thoroughly. Add sifted flour gradually, kneading the last portion into dough by hand until mixture "cracks" but does not crumble. Roll out dough on lightly floured board to 1/4-inch thickness. Decorate as desired. Place on ungreased baking sheet and bake 5 to 7 minutes.

RAISIN BARS

$1^1/_4$ cups all-purpose flour
$1^1/_4$ cups brown sugar, packed
$^1/_2$ cup butter
   2 eggs
$1^1/_2$ tsp. baking powder
$^1/_4$ tsp. salt
   1 cup chopped raisins
$^1/_2$ cup candied chopped cherries
$^1/_2$ cup flaked coconut
$^1/_2$ cup chopped nuts

Blend 1 cup of flour, $^1/_4$ cup brown sugar and butter together well. Press into 9-inch square pan. Bake 10 minutes at 350 degrees F. Set aside. Beat eggs well. Add remaining 1 cup sugar gradually. Sift remaining $^1/_4$ cup flour, baking powder and salt together. Add to egg mixture. Stir in raisins, cherries, coconut and nuts. Spoon over baked base. Return to oven and bake 30-35 minutes. Cool. Spread the following icing if desired: $^1/_4$ cup butter, 1 cup icing sugar, 1 tbsp. vanilla. Mix well.

RICH CHRISTMAS COOKIES

   1 cup butter
   1 cup sugar
   2 large eggs
$^1/_2$ tsp. cream of tartar
$^1/_2$ tsp. salt
   1 tsp. vanilla
$2^1/_2$ cups flour
   1 tsp. soda

Cream butter and sugar. Add eggs and vanilla. Mix in dry ingredients. Roll $^1/_8$ inch thick and cut with cookie cutters. Sprinkle with colored sugar. Bake on greased cookie sheet at 350 degrees F. for 10 minutes. May be iced after cooling. (For a change of flavor, add 1 tsp. grated lemon rind and 1 tsp. lemon juice.)

Mom's Helpers

To shell nuts so they come out whole, soak the nuts overnight in salted water before cracking them.

RUM BALLS

3 cups crushed graham wafers
1 cup icing sugar
1 heaping tbsp. cocoa
$^1/_2$ cup finely chopped walnuts
$^1/_4$ cup brandy or dark rum
$^1/_4$ cup corn syrup
$1^1/_4$ tsp. water to moisten

Mix wafers, icing sugar, cocoa and walnuts together. Add brandy or rum, corn syrup and water. Mix well and let stand for 15 minutes. Mixture should hold together when shaped into balls. If too dry, add more brandy or rum, 1 tsp. at a time until the right consistency is reached. Roll balls in finely shaved unsweetened chocolate bits. Chill before serving.

TEMPTING ICEBOX COOKIES

$1^3/_4$ cups butter
2 cups brown sugar
1 cup granulated sugar
4 large eggs
4 to 5 cups flour (dough should be stiff)
1 tbsp. baking powder
2 tbsp. cinnamon
$^1/_2$ tsp. cloves
$^1/_4$ tsp. allspice
2 cups whole walnuts
1 tbsp. vanilla

Blend butter and sugars together with electric mixer. Add eggs, one at a time, plus vanilla. Sift all dry ingredients together and add to above mixture. Add nuts. Roll dough into desired size rolls. Wrap in wax paper and refrigerate overnight. Slice thin and bake in 350 degrees F. oven for 15 to 20 minutes or until they begin to brown. (This dough may be frozen and keeps well for several weeks.)

Mom's Helpers

If a bit of egg yolk gets into the whites while you separate eggs, scoop out the yolk with half the eggshell. The shell acts as a magnet with small bits of yolk.

TRUE BUTTERSCOTCH COOKIES

2¹/₂ cups sifted flour
   1 tsp. baking soda
  ¹/₂ tsp. baking powder
  ¹/₂ tsp. salt
   1 tbsp. vinegar
    Cereal cream
1¹/₂ cups brown sugar, packed
  ¹/₂ cup butter
   2 eggs
   1 tsp. vanilla
  ²/₃ cup chopped walnuts
    Browned frosting (recipe follows)
    Walnut halves

Sift together flour, baking soda, baking powder and salt; set aside. Place vinegar in glass measuring cup. Add enough cream to make 1 cup liquid; set aside. Cream together butter and brown sugar until light and fluffy. Add eggs, one at a time, beating well after each addition. Mix in vanilla. Add dry ingredients alternately with cereal cream mixture to creamed sugar mixture, mixing well. Stir in nuts. Drop mixture by rounded tablespoonfuls, about 2¹/₂ inches apart, onto greased baking sheets. Bake at 350 degrees F. 10 to 12 minutes or until lightly browned. Cool. Yield 4 dozen. Frost with Browned frosting if desired.

BROWNED FROSTING

Melt ¹/₂ cup butter in saucepan over medium heat. Stir constantly until butter stops bubbling and turns nutty-brown in color. DO NOT SCORCH. Combine butter with 2 cups sifted icing sugar and 2 tbsp. boiling water. Beat until smooth and creamy, using a spoon. If icing thickens while icing the cookies, add ¹/₂ tsp. of hot water until desired consistency is acquired.

Mom's Helpers
Prevent boiled icing from becoming sugary and crusty by adding a few drops of vinegar to the icing as it cooks — you won't taste the vinegar.

RUBIES AND EMERALDS

    1 cup butter
 $^1/_3$ cup sugar
    1 whole large egg
    1 egg yolk
    3 cups flour
       Pinch of salt
       Mint jelly
       Strawberry jelly
       Nuts, finely chopped
       Coconut, finely chopped
    1 large egg white, lightly beaten

Place the first six ingredients into the food processor and mix until the dough forms into a soft ball. If mixing by hand, mix until a soft smooth dough forms. Shape dough in balls $^3/_4$ inch in diameter. Place the chopped coconut into one bowl and the chopped nuts into a second bowl. Dip one half of the small balls of dough into the beaten egg white, then into the coconut. Dip the remaining small balls into the beaten egg white, then into the chopped nuts. Place on a greased cookie sheet. Make a finger dent in the middle of each little ball and bake for 25 to 30 minutes at 325 degrees F. Set aside to cool. When cookies are cooled, fill each with green or red jelly. Red and green maraschino cherries can be substituted for the jellies, if so desired.

QUICK COFFEE CAKE

    2 tbsp. butter, melted
 $^3/_4$ cup brown sugar
    1 tsp. cinnamon
 $1^3/_4$ cups flour
    3 tsp. baking powder
 $^1/_2$ tsp. salt
 $^2/_3$ cup sugar
 $^1/_3$ cup butter
    1 egg
    1 cup milk
    1 tsp. vanilla

Grease an 8 x 8 inch pan thoroughly. In separate bowl, melt 2 tbsp. butter. Stir in brown sugar and cinnamon. Set aside for topping of cake. Measure flour without sifting into large bowl; add baking powder, salt, and sugar and stir to blend thoroughly. Cut in the butter with pastry blender. Make a hollow and add egg, milk and vanilla. Break egg yolk and stir milk and egg together in hollow; then combine with dry ingredients, mixing just until moistened. Turn into pan and sprinkle with brown sugar and cinnamon mixture. Bake in 375 degree F. oven for 30 to 35 minutes. Serve warm.

YUM YUM CAKE

$^1/_2$ **cup chopped walnuts**
$^1/_2$ **cup dates**
  1 **cup raisins**
  1 **cup boiling water**
  1 **tsp. soda**

Mix the above together and allow to stand while preparing the rest of the cake as follows:

  1 **cup sugar**
$^1/_2$ **cup butter**
  1 **tsp. vanilla**
$1^1/_2$ **cups flour**
  1 **tsp. cinnamon**

Blend sugar and butter until fluffy. Stir in cinnamon and vanilla. Add flour and first mixture. Pour into an 8 × 8 inch square pan, and bake at 375 degrees F. for 30 to 40 minutes until done. When cool, frost with the following caramel frosting. Bring to a boil $^3/_4$ cup brown sugar and $^1/_3$ cup milk in a saucepan. Remove saucepan from heat and beat in enough icing sugar (about 1 cup) to make a creamy icing. Stir in 1 tsp. vanilla. Work fast and spread immediately over cake as the frosting sets quickly.

Mom's Helpers

Sear meat before salting it. Salt tends to draw out some juices from the meat.

Help keep cauliflower white while it cooks. Add a little milk to the water in which the cauliflower is being cooked.

For a dramatic dessert, make a small cavity in the top of a cake, pudding or mound of ice cream just large enough to hold one half of an eggshell. Set the egg shell in place, fill $^2/_3$ of the shell with a heated liqueur, then ignite the liqueur.

ICELANDIC LAYER CAKE

      1 cup soft butter
  1¹/₂ cups fruit sugar
      2 eggs
      1 cup sifted flour
      1 tsp. baking powder
         Pinch of salt
      3 tbsp. light cream
      1 tbsp. almond extract
   ¹/₄ tsp. ground cardamom
      3 cups sifted flour
         Prune filling (recipe follows)

Heat oven to 350 degrees F. Grease two 9-inch layer cake pans. Cream butter thoroughly. Start adding sugar gradually and cream well after each addition. Add eggs, one at a time and beat well after each. Sift the 1 cup flour, baking powder and salt together into mixture and blend well. Add cream, almond extract, and cardamom and beat well again. Blend in remaining flour, working dough very well with a spoon or your hands. Spread 1 cup of the mixture carefully inside each of the layer pans. Pat dough so it is as even as possible. Bake about 15 minutes or until lightly browned. Cool a few minutes and slip carefully out of pans onto cake rack. Let pans cool, wipe with paper towelling, grease again. Repeat spreading and baking of dough. Repeat these steps once more except this time you will have just enough dough for one pan — 5 rounds in all. Stack layers with a thin layer of Prune filling between each two. Ice top with a thin layer of butter icing if desired. Cut in wedges or slices to serve. For best results, chill the filled cake for 2 hours before cutting.

Prune Filling:

      1 lb. prunes
   ³/₄ cup sugar
   ¹/₂ cup liquid (see below)
      1 tbsp. cinnamon
      1 tbsp. vanilla

Into a saucepan pour in two cups of water, then add the prunes, and cook on top of the stove until done, about 20 minutes. Drain prunes, saving ¹/₂ cup of liquid. Set aside. Stone if required, and put prunes through a food chopper. Return prunes to saucepan. Add sugar, the ¹/₂ cup cooking liquid and cinnamon. Bring to a boil and cook, stirring constantly, until mixture becomes quite thick, about 5 minutes. Remove from heat and stir in vanilla. Cook to lukewarm and spread between layers of cake as directed above.

Mom's Helpers

When doubling a recipe — do NOT double the salt. Increase it by one-half only.

DELICIOUS BANANA COFFEE CAKE

1¹/₂ cups cake flour
³/₄ tsp. baking powder
³/₄ tsp. salt
³/₄ cup mashed ripe banana
1 tsp. vanilla
2 egg yolks
¹/₄ cup brown sugar
³/₄ tsp. baking soda
³/₄ cup brown sugar
¹/₄ cup salad oil
¹/₄ cup buttermilk
¹/₄ cup buttermilk, again
2 beaten egg whites
¹/₂ cup chopped nuts

Mix flour, ³/₄ cup brown sugar, baking powder, baking soda, and salt into a bowl. Add bananas, oil, ¹/₄ cup buttermilk and vanilla. Beat at high speed for 1 minute. Now add remaining ¹/₄ cup buttermilk and egg yolks. Beat at high speed for 1 minute. Beat egg whites until frothy, then add ¹/₄ cup of brown sugar to whites. Beat until soft peaks form. Add chopped nuts to flour mixture. Gently fold flour mixture into egg white mixture. Pour into 9-inch square greased and floured pan. Bake for 40 minutes at 350 degrees F. or until cake springs back when lightly touched at center. Ice with one of the following toppings:

1 cup brown sugar
3 tbsp. butter
3 tbsp. cream

Combine the three ingredients into a saucepan and boil for 3 minutes, stirring constantly. Remove from heat and beat vigorously until light and of spreading consistency.

OR:

5 tbsp. brown sugar
1 tbsp. butter
3 tbsp. milk
Icing sugar as needed

Mix first 3 ingredients in a saucepan and bring to a boil. Cool slightly. Add icing sugar until desired thickness is reached and spread.

Mom's Helpers

There is no nutritional or flavour difference between white-shelled and brown-shelled eggs.

PUMPKIN CAKE

        4 eggs
        2 cups sugar
        1 cup vegetable oil
        2 cups pumpkin
        3 cups flour
        2 tsp. baking powder
        2 tsp. baking soda
    $^1/_2$ tsp. salt
    $^1/_2$ tsp. cinnamon
        6 oz. chocolate chips
    $^1/_2$ tsp. allspice
    $^1/_4$ tsp. cloves
    $^1/_4$ tsp. ginger

Cream eggs and sugar. Add the remaining ingredients, combine well. Pour into a large tube or bundt pan. Bake at 350 degrees F. for 1 hour and 10 minutes. Ice with the following:

        5 tbsp. flour
        1 cup milk
        1 cup butter
        1 cup icing sugar
    $1^1/_2$ tsp. vanilla

Put flour into milk in saucepan. Put on stove, mix until smooth and cook over medium heat until thick. (Can be lumpy) This mixture burns easily, so watch carefully. Take off stove and cool mixture until ICE COLD. In another bowl cream butter, sugar and vanilla with a beater. When first mixture is cold, take beaters out of icing sugar mixture. Add 1 tbsp. at a time to flour mixture. Beat well after each addition. The more beating, the fluffier the icing will be. It should resemble whipping cream for lightness.

Mom's Helpers

To protect your knees while you do jobs that require kneeling, sew a pocket on each knee of an old pair of slacks. Insert sponge in each pocket and you have knee cushions that move with you. Remove sponges before laundering slacks.

To determine whether an egg is hard-cooked, spin it. If it spins round and round, it is hard-cooked. If it wobbles and will not spin, it is a raw egg.

FRUIT COCKTAIL CAKE

$1^1/_2$ cups white sugar
  2 tsp. baking soda
  2 eggs
  2 cups flour
$^1/_2$ tsp. salt
 14 oz. can fruit cocktail with juice

Beat eggs slightly. Add all ingredients except flour. Add flour and bake in a 9 × 13 inch greased pan for 45 minutes at 350 degrees F.

Icing:

$^3/_4$ cup white sugar
$^1/_2$ cup cream
$^1/_2$ cup butter
  1 tsp. vanilla

Boil all ingredients except vanilla. Add vanilla, and pour over hot cake. Makes a lot, but use all of it. Serve warm with ice cream or whipped cream. Keeps refrigerated for several days.

APPLESAUCE CAKE

$^1/_2$ cup soft butter
$^3/_4$ cup liquid honey
  2 cups sifted flour
  1 tsp. soda
$^1/_4$ tsp. salt
$^1/_2$ tsp. nutmeg
$^1/_2$ tsp. cinnamon
$^1/_4$ tsp. cloves
  1 cup canned sweetened applesauce
  1 cup seedless raisins
     Broiled icing

Heat oven to 350 degrees F. Grease a 9-inch square cake pan. Cream butter thoroughly. Add honey gradually and beat well after each addition. Sift flour, soda, salt and spices together and add to first mixture alternately with applesauce, blending well after each addition. Stir in raisins. Pour batter into prepared pan and bake about 35 minutes or until top springs back when touched lightly in the center. Remove cake from oven and turn on the broiler. Spread hot cake with broiled icing and slip low under broiler (middle of the oven) just until topping bubbles and browns lightly. Cool in pan.

Broiled Icing:

 ¹/₄ cup soft butter
 ¹/₃ cup liquid honey
 ¹/₄ tsp. cinnamon
 ¹/₂ cup flaked coconut
 ¹/₂ cup chopped walnuts

Cream butter, honey and cinnamon together. Stir in coconut and walnuts.
Spread on cake.

CHOCOLATE TORTE

 1 cup butter
 ²/₃ cup cocoa
 1 cup sugar
 8 egg yolks
 8 egg whites, beaten stiff
 1 cup ground walnuts
 ¹/₂ cup bread crumbs
 1 tsp. vanilla

Cream butter well. Add vanilla. Mix the cocoa with the sugar. Add 1 egg yolk
and 1 tbsp. sugar-cocoa mixture at a time, mixing very well after each addition.
After all egg yolks and mixture are worked in, very carefully fold in ground
nuts. Fold in bread crumbs. Set aside. Whip egg whites until stiff. Fold in
creamed mixture very carefully. Grease three 9-inch round pans and line the
bottoms with wax or brown paper. Divide mixture evenly and pour into pans.
Bake at 350 degrees F. for 30 minutes. Cool for 10 minutes and remove from
pans. Fill with the following filling:

Butter-Nut Filling:

 1 cup butter, whipped
 3-4 tbsp. thick cream
 2 cups ground walnuts
 ¹/₂ cup bread crumbs
 1¹/₂ cups icing sugar
 ¹/₂ tsp. vanilla

Mix well and spread between the layers. Chill for 2 hours before cutting.

Mom's Helpers

*Get more juice from citrus fruits by heating the lemons, oranges, or grapefruit in the
oven for just a few minutes before extracting the juice.*

RICH DARK FRUIT CAKE

          2 cups seeded raisins
          2 cups seedless raisins
$1^1/_2$ cups currants
$1^1/_2$ cups candied cherries, halved
$1^1/_2$ cups chopped dates
$1^1/_2$ cups candied fruit
$1^1/_2$ cups pecans (halves)
          1 cups finely chopped pared, cored apple
      $^1/_2$ cup red wine
$2^3/_4$ cups regular flour
          1 tsp. baking powder
$1^1/_2$ tsp. cinnamon
$1^1/_2$ tsp. ginger
$1^1/_2$ tsp. mace
          1 tsp. ground cloves
      $^1/_2$ tsp. salt
          1 cup butter
          1 cup brown sugar, firmly packed
          6 eggs
      $^1/_4$ cup light molasses
          2 squares (2 oz.) unsweetened melted chocolate

The night before: into a large mixing bowl mix the first 8 ingredients (fruit and nuts) together. Pour the wine over the fruit and occasionally stir to get all fruit soaking into the wine.

Next day: line 9-inch or 10-inch tube pan with two thicknesses of buttered brown paper. Combine fruits, nuts and fresh apple in large bowl. Dredge with $^1/_4$ cup of the flour. Measure $2^1/_2$ cups flour (without sifting) onto square waxed paper. Add baking powder, spices and salt; stir well to blend. Cream butter and brown sugar together. Beat in molasses and melted chocolate. Add blended dry ingredients to creamed mixture, combining well. Stir in fruit-nut mixture until well mixed. Spread batter evenly in prepared pan. Bake at 275 degrees F. for about $2^1/_2$ hours, or until cake tester inserted into center comes out clean. Let cool completely in pan on wire rack. Remove from pan, peel off paper and wrap in foil. Store in airtight container or in refrigerator for several weeks.

TO GLAZE AND DECORATE CAKE: Combine 1 cup sugar, $^1/_2$ cup water and $^1/_3$ cup light corn syrup in saucepan. Stir over low heat until sugar is dissolved, then boil to firm ball stage (240 degrees F. on candy thermometer). Brush hot glaze over cooled cake. Decorate top with candied cherries and nuts and brush cake again with hot glaze. Let dry thoroughly before wrapping and storing. Marzipan fruit can be placed around the top of the cake before serving.

Mom's Helpers

Store chopped nuts in the refrigerator. Packed in airtight jars or plastic containers, the nutsmeats will keep perfectly fresh for months.

SIMNEL CAKE

Almond paste:

- $^1/_2$ **lb. blanched almonds**
- 1 **cup fine granulated sugar**
- 3 **cups sifted icing sugar**
- 2 **eggs**
- 1 **tsp. almond extract**

Chop almond finely in a blender or food processor; mix in sugars, eggs and almond extract. Knead until dough-like, adding a little icing sugar if needed. Set aside.

Cake:

- 1 **cup currants, washed and dried**
- $^1/_4$ **cup chopped mixed candied peels**
- 1 **tsp. grated lemon rind**
- $2^1/_4$ **cup sifted all-purpose flour**
- 2 **tsp. baking powder**
- $^1/_2$ **tsp. salt**
- 1 **cup butter**
- $1^1/_4$ **cups fine granulated sugar**
- 5 **eggs**

Combine currants, peels, and lemon rind in bowl. Sift flour, baking powder and salt over fruit; mix well. Cream butter and gradually blend in sugar. Add eggs, one at a time, beating in well after each addition. Stir in flour mixture; combine well. Spread half of batter in a greased 9-inch square or 10-inch round cake pan, lined in bottom with greased waxed paper. Roll out $^1/_2$ of the almond paste 1-inch smaller than pan and place over batter; cover with remaining batter. Bake in a slow oven, 300 degrees F., about $1^3/_4$ hours. Cool cake in pan for about 10 minutes; then turn out on rack, peel off paper, turn cake top-side up and allow to cool completely. Brush top of cake with egg white and top with remaining almond paste, rolled out to fit the cake.

EASY FUDGE ICING

- 2 **cups sugar**
- $^1/_4$ **cup corn syrup**
- $^1/_2$ **cup milk**
- $^1/_2$ **cup butter**
- 2 **squares (2 oz.) unsweetened chocolate, cut up**
- $^1/_4$ **tsp. salt**
- 1 **tsp. vanilla**

Mix sugar, corn syrup, milk, butter, chocolate and salt in a saucepan. Put over low heat and stir until chocolate and butter begin to melt. Bring to a boil, stirring constantly. Boil 1 minute. Remove from heat and beat until lukewarm. Stir in vanilla and continue beating until the icing is the right consistency to spread.

Light Cake Brownies, Page 72, icelandic Layer Cake, Page 80
Dark Chocolate Cake, Page 94, with Chocolate Butter Cream, Page 93

CREAMY NUT ICING

1/4 cup butter
4 tsp. flour
Pinch of salt
1/4 cup milk
1³/₄ cups sifted icing sugar
1 tsp. vanilla
1/3 cup chopped walnuts

Melt butter in small saucepan. Sprinkle in flour and salt and stir to blend. Remove from heat and stir in milk all at once. Turn heat down to moderate and cook mixture, stirring constantly, until thick and smooth. Remove from heat and stir in sugar and vanilla. Set pan in ice water and stir until frosting is thick enough to spread. Stir in nuts and ice any chocolate cake.

DATE UP-SIDE DOWN PUDDING CAKE

1 cup pitted and chopped up dates
2 tbsp. butter
1 cup boiling water
1 egg
1¹/₂ cups flour
1/4 cup sugar
1/4 cup brown sugar
1 tsp. soda
1/2 tsp. baking powder
1/2 tsp. salt
1/2 cup walnuts

Preheat oven to 375 degrees F. Arrange dates into bottom of a 9-inch round pan. Add 2 tbsp. butter. Pour one cup boiling water over dates. Stir up date mixture to soften dates. Add remaining ingredients to mixture in pan. Beat until thoroughly blended — about 2 minutes. Scrape bottom and sides frequently while blending. Smooth batter evenly in pan. Sprinkle with ³/₄ cup brown sugar. Slowly pour 1¹/₂ cups boiling water over all. Bake for about 40-45 minutes. Serve with ice cream. Serves 8.

Mom's Helpers

Make cranberry sauce when cranberries are in season and freeze without sugar for later use.

CHOCOLATE MARBLE CAKE

 $^3/_4$ cup soft butter
 $1^1/_2$ cups sugar
 3 eggs
 $2^1/_2$ cups all-purpose flour
 1 tsp. salt
 3 tsp. baking powder
 1 cup less 2 tbsp. milk
 $1^1/_2$ tsp. vanilla
 4 oz. unsweetened chocolate

Cream butter and sugar together until fluffy. Add one egg at a time, beating for 1 minutes after each addition. Sift flour with the salt and baking powder, add alternately with milk and flavoring to creamed mixture. Stir just enough to blend. Place 6 heaping tbsp. of batter in another bowl. Melt the chocolate, cool and add to the 6 tbsp. of batter. Blend well. Drop by spoonfuls of chocolate mixture at intervals with the white batter, then run a knife through the batter in a wavy fashion, creating the marble effect. Bake at 350 degrees F. for 40 to 45 minutes. Cool on rack. Ice with Easy Fudge Icing if desired.

DATE CHOCOLATE CHIP CAKE

 $^3/_4$ cup butter
 $1^1/_4$ cups boiling water
 1 cup chopped dates
 1 cup sugar
 2 eggs
 2 cups sifted all-purpose flour
 1 tsp. soda
 $^1/_2$ tsp. salt
 1 tbsp. cocoa

Topping:

 $^1/_4$ cup sugar
 $^1/_2$ cup chopped nuts
 6 oz. pkg. semi sweet chocolate chips

Pour boiling water over dates in small bowl. Cool. Cream butter and sugar. Add eggs and beat well. Sift flour with soda, salt, and cocoa. Add to butter mixture alternately with date mixture, adding the dry ingredients first and last. Pour batter into 13 x 9½ x 2 inch greased pan. Sprinkle topping ingredients over batter. Bake at 350 degrees F. for 35-40 minutes.

SURPRISE COFFEE CAKE

$^1/_2$ cup sugar
1 tbsp. cocoa
1 tsp. cinnamon
$^1/_2$ cup chopped walnuts
$1^3/_4$ cups sifted flour
2 tsp. baking powder
$^3/_4$ tsp. baking soda
$^1/_3$ cup butter
$^2/_3$ cup sugar
2 eggs, unbeaten
$^3/_4$ cup thick sour cream

Grease a 9-inch tube pan or an 8×8 inch square pan. Combine sugar, cinnamon, cocoa, and walnuts; set aside. In another bowl, mix flour with baking soda and baking powder. In a large bowl cream butter until light and gradually add sugar, beating well after each addition. Blend in flour mixture alternately with sour cream. Into prepared pan pour half the batter; top with cocoa mixture; spread remaining batter over cocoa filling. Bake 35 to 40 minutes at 375 degrees F. Cool 10 minutes in pan; remove and finish cooling on wire rack.

HOT WATER GINGERBREAD

$^1/_2$ cup boiling water
$^1/_3$ cup butter
$^1/_4$ cup sugar
$^1/_2$ cup molasses
1 egg
$1^1/_2$ cups sifted all-purpose flour
1 tsp. soda
$^1/_2$ tsp. salt
2 tsp. ginger
Icing sugar or sweetened whipped cream

Grease a 9-inch square cake pan. Put butter in a mixing bowl. Add boiling water to butter and stir until melted. Stir in sugar, molasses and egg. Beat hard until sugar is dissolved and mixture is well blended. Sift flour, soda, salt and ginger together into first mixture. Beat hard to blend well. Pour batter into prepared pan. Bake about 20 minutes or until top springs back when touched lightly in the center. Serve warm with icing sugar sifted over top or with sweetened whipped cream.

GINGERBREAD SQUARE

- 1/3 cup butter
- 1/2 cup brown sugar
- 3/4 cup molasses
- 1 egg, beaten
- 2 cups sifted all-purpose flour
- 1 1/4 tsp. ginger
- 1/4 tsp. cinnamon
- 1/4 tsp. cloves
- 1/2 tsp. salt
- 2 tsp. soda
- 1 cup boiling water

Grease a 9-inch square cake pan. Cream butter in a bowl. Add sugar and continue creaming for 2 minutes. Beat in molasses and egg. Sift flour, ginger, cinnamon, cloves and salt together into first mixture. Add soda to boiling water and stir to blend. Add to previous mixture and beat to blend. Batter will be fairly thin. Pour into prepared pan and bake 30-35 minutes at 350 degrees F. Center should spring back when touched lightly in the center. Serve warm or cold with whipped cream.

SOUR CREAM CAKE

- 1 egg
- 1 cup brown sugar, packed
- 1 cup thick sour cream
- 3/4 cup flaked coconut
- 2 cups sifted all-purpose flour
- 1 tsp. soda
- 1/2 tsp. baking power
- 1/4 tsp. salt
  Caramel Icing

Grease a 9-inch square pan. In a large bowl beat egg. Add sugar gradually, beating well after each addition. Stir in sour cream and coconut. Sift flour, soda, baking powder, and salt together into mixture and beat well — about 2 minutes. Spread batter into the greased pan and bake for 25-30 minutes or until the top springs back when touched lightly in the center at 375 degrees F.

Caramel Icing:

- 1 cup brown sugar, packed
- 1/3 cup butter
- 1/3 cup milk
- 1 cup icing sugar

Boil brown sugar, butter, and milk hard in a small saucepan, stirring constantly for 3 minutes. Cool to lukewarm. Stir in icing sugar and continue stirring until the right spreading consistency is reached.

CELEBRATION GINGERBREAD

1³/₄ cups all-purpose flour
1¹/₂ tsp. baking powder
 ³/₄ tsp. soda
 ³/₄ tsp. salt
1¹/₂ tsp. ginger
1¹/₂ tsp. cinnamon
 ¹/₄ tsp. ground cloves
 ¹/₂ cup butter
 ¹/₂ cup brown sugar
 ³/₄ cup molasses
  2 eggs
 ³/₄ cup boiling water

Measure flour into a large bowl. Add baking powder, soda, salt and spices. Stir well to blend. Cream butter and brown sugar well. Add molasses and eggs and beat well. Add blended dry ingredients gradually, mixing well. Add boiling water and mix quickly to a smooth batter. Spread in greased and lightly floured 9-inch square pan. Bake at 350 degrees F. for 40-45 minutes. Serve with the following topping:

  1 cup whipping cream
  1 tbsp. sugar
  1 tsp. vanilla
    Pinch of salt
  1 cup drained canned fruit cocktail

Whip cream, sugar, vanilla, and salt together until stiff. Fold in drained fruits. Serves 6.

RAISIN GINGERBREAD

 ¹/₂ cup sugar
 ¹/₂ cup butter
  1 egg
  1 cup molasses
2¹/₂ cups sifted flour
1¹/₂ tsp. soda
  1 tsp. cinnamon
  1 tsp. ginger
 ¹/₂ tsp. cloves
 ¹/₂ tsp. salt
  1 cup hot water
  1 cup raisins

Wash raisins then pour 2 cups boiling water over them while preparing the remaining batter. Allow raisins to soften. In a large bowl cream butter and sugar. Add beaten egg, molasses, and then the dry ingredients in the order given. Add 1 cup hot water last and beat until smooth, then add the raisins. Pour into an 8-inch square pan and bake 35 to 40 minutes at 375 degrees F.

CHOCOLATE POUND CAKE

1 cup soft butter
2 cups granulated sugar
2¹/₂ cups all-purpose flour
¹/₂ tsp. salt
1 tsp. baking powder
1 tsp. vanilla
4 eggs
1 cup buttermilk
3 oz. unsweetened chocolate
1 tbsp. instant coffee
1 cup chopped nuts

Cream together butter and sugar until very light and creamy — about 3 minutes with electric beater. In a separate bowl sift together the flour, salt and baking powder and add to the creamed mixture. Stir in vanilla. Add the eggs, one at a time, beating well after each addition. Add the buttermilk and mix thoroughly. Melt the chocolate over hot water, stir in the instant coffee. Cool slightly. Add to the batter, mix well and fold in the chopped nuts. Bake in a greased and floured 9 x 5 x 3-inch loaf pan, lined with wax paper, in a 350 degree F. oven for 55 minutes. Remove from pan and cool on wire rack.

LIGHT CARROT CAKE

1 cup sugar
¹/₂ cup butter
¹/₂ cup salad oil
4 eggs
1 cup all-purpose flour
1 cup whole wheat flour
1¹/₂ tsp. baking soda
1 tsp. salt
2 tsp. cinnamon
2 cups grated raw carrot
1¹/₂ cup grated apple
1 cup raisins
¹/₂ cup chopped walnuts

Blend together sugar, butter, oil and eggs. Beat until thick. Sift together dry ingredients, and combine with egg mixture. Add carrot, apple, raisins, and nuts and blend. Pour into a greased and lined with wax paper pan 9 x 13 x 2 inches. Bake 35-40 minutes at 350 degrees F. Frost with cream cheese frosting.

Cream Cheese Frosting:

> 1 (4-oz.) package cream cheese
> 1/4 cup butter
> 1 cup icing sugar
> 1 tsp. vanilla

Beat cream cheese and butter until fluffy. Beat in icing sugar and vanilla until well combined and spread over the cake.

CHOCOLATE BUTTER CREAM

> 6 oz. semisweet chocolate
> 1/2 cup soft unsalted butter
> 1 egg yolk
> 1 tsp. vanilla
> 1 tsp. instant coffee

Melt chocolate over hot water. When soft, stir until smooth. Allow to cool. In a separate bowl, cream the butter with the egg yolk, vanilla, and instant coffee. Beat in the cooled chocolate and stir until creamy and fluffy. If the melted chocolate is added to the butter while it is still too hot, the butter will not stay creamy. Refrigerate until thick enough, beat and spread on cake. This topping does not dry or get hard.

ONE-STEP CHOCOLATE FUDGE CAKE

> 1/3 cup salad oil or melted shortening
> 2 oz. cocoa
> 1 egg
> 1 cup sugar
> 1 1/4 cups cake flour
> 1/2 tsp. soda
> 1/2 tsp. baking powder
> 1/2 tsp. salt
> 1/2 tsp. vanilla
> 3/4 cup water
> 1/2 cup semisweet chocolate chips
> 1/4 cup walnut pieces

Preheat oven to 350 degrees F. In a 9-inch square pan combine all the ingredients in the order given. Beat with a fork until smooth and creamy — about 2 minutes. Scrape sides and bottom with rubber spatula. Spread batter evenly in the pan. Sprinkle with 1/2 cup chocolate chips and walnut pieces over top of the batter. Bake for 30-35 minutes. Cool in pan.

DARK CHOCOLATE CAKE

- $^1/_2$ cup butter
- 4 egg yolks
- $1^3/_4$ cups granulated sugar
- 2 cups all-purpose flour
- $^1/_2$ cup cocoa
- 1 tsp. baking powder
- $^1/_2$ tsp. baking soda
- $^1/_4$ tsp. salt
- $1^1/_4$ cups milk
- 4 egg whites, stiffly beaten
- 1 tsp. vanilla
- 1 cup whipping cream
- $^1/_3$ cup icing sugar
- $^1/_8$ tsp. mace

Cream butter until light, gradually add sugar and beat until well mixed. Add egg yolks, one at a time, and beat for 10 minutes with electric mixer. After this length of beating in air, the mixture will look very light in color and very light in texture. In a separate bowl, sift together flour, cocoa, baking powder, soda and salt. Add alternately with milk to the creamed mixture, and beat for 1 minute until smooth. Fold in egg whites and vanilla. Pour into two 10-inch cake pans which have been greased and floured. Bake at 325 degrees F. for 50-60 minutes or until done. Cool. Whip cream, add the mace and sugar. Fill and ice the cooled cake with cream mixture. Put 1 tsp. cocoa in a small sieve and sprinkle lightly over cream, just enough to speckle.

YUMMY FRUIT BARS

- $^3/_4$ cup softened butter
- 1 scant cup brown sugar
- $^1/_2$ tsp. salt
- $^3/_4$ tsp. baking soda
- $1^3/_4$ cups all-purpose flour
- $1^1/_2$ cups rolled oats

Heat oven to 375 degrees F. Grease a $7^1/_2 \times 11 \times 2$ inch pan.
Using an electric mixer, cream butter and sugar for 2 minutes, until light and fluffy. Add salt, baking soda and flour. Beat enough to mix well. Add rolled oats, mix well. Mixture will be coarse and crumbly.

Press one half of the mixture evenly into the pan. Spread cooled filling carefully. Cover with the remaining mixture and press even lightly. Bake for 30 to 35 minutes or until lightly browned. Cool. Cut into $2 \times 1^1/_2$ inch bars.

Fruit Filling:

Mix 2 cups of fresh fruit with ¼ cup sugar into a saucepan. Add 1½ cups water to which 2 level tbsp. of cornstarch has been stirred into. Cook until the mixture reaches a boil and the fruit is soft. Cool and spread.

Jelly Filling:

Dissolve 2 tbsp. cornstarch into ¼ cup of cold water. Pour into a saucepan. Add 1 cup of jam or jelly. Add 1¼ cup water. Stir well. Heat until mixture boils and takes on a translucent appearance. Cool and spread.

POPPY SEED CHARM CAKE

    1   cup milk
   ½   cup poppy seeds
   ¾   cup soft butter
  1½   cups granulated sugar
    4   eggs
    2   cups sifted all purpose flour
    3   tsp. baking powder
    1   tsp. salt
    2   cups milk
   ½   cup granulated sugar
    4   tbsp. cornstarch
   ¼   tsp. salt
  1½   tsp. vanilla

Grease three 9-inch layer cake pans; line bottom with waxed paper. Set aside. Scald milk and add poppy seed to hot milk. Set aside to soak and cool. In a mixing bowl cream butter and gradually add 1½ cups sugar, beating until fluffy, about 3 minutes. Add 2 egg yolks. Beat another 2 minutes. Sift flour with baking powder and 1 tsp. salt. Add alternately with cooled milk-poppy seed mixture, blending after each addition. Beat 3 egg whites until stiff but not dry. Fold in. Pour into prepared pans, spread evenly, and bake for 25 to 30 minutes at 350 degrees F. oven. Test by inserting a toothpick into the center of the cake. Remove to cooling racks for 10 minutes. Remove paper when cool.
Prepare filling: Scald the 2 cups milk in double boiler over boiling water. Beat one egg yolk with one whole egg. Combine the ½ cup sugar, cornstarch and ¼ tsp. salt. Blend into beaten egg. Stir a little scalded milk into egg mixture, stir into scalded milk. Cook over boiling water, stirring constantly, until smooth and thickened. Pour into bowl to cool. Stir in vanilla. Stir while filling is cooling. Spread filling between layers and frost top with your favourite butter icing — using about 3 cups icing sugar. Decorate with crushed walnuts.

Mom's Helpers

Never cover the entire baking rack or heating elements on the floor of the oven with foil. This could cause poor heat circulation, uneven baking and possible damage to the range.

DESSERTS
and
BEVERAGES

NO-BAKE CHEESECAKE

3 tbsp. melted butter
$^3/_4$ cup graham crumbs
2 tbsp. sugar
$^1/_4$ tsp. cinnamon
$^1/_4$ tsp. nutmeg

Combine all ingredients. Press $^1/_2$ cup of the mixture into an 8-inch spring form pan or 8-cup loaf pan which has been lined with wax paper.

3 envelopes unflavoured gelatin
1 cup milk
2 eggs, separated
3 cups cottage cheese, creamed
$^3/_4$ cup frozen lemonade concentrate
$^1/_4$ cup sugar
1 cup heavy cream, whipped

Sprinkle gelatin on milk in a large saucepan. Add egg yolks, stir well. Place over low heat stirring constantly until gelatin dissolves and mixture thickens slightly. Remove from heat. Put cottage cheese through food processor then add the lemon concentrate. Whip for 30 seconds, then stir into gelatin mixture. Beat egg whites until stiff; gradually add sugar and beat stiff. Fold gelatin mixture into the whites, then fold in whipped cream. Turn into a prepared pan; sprinkle with reserved crumb mixture. Chill until firm — 2 to 3 hours. Serves 10.

Mom's Helpers

For a smooth creamy cheesecake do not over bake it. Even if the center does not seem quite set, it will solidify as the cake cools.

OLD FASHIONED FRUIT PUDDING

1 cup molasses
1 cup currants
1 cup raisins
1 cup ground suet
3 cups sifted flour
2 tsp. baking powder
1/2 tsp. salt
1 tsp. cloves
1 tsp. cinnamon
1/4 tsp. allspice
1 1/2 cups milk
1 cup chopped nuts

Combine molasses, currants, raisins and suet. Mix dry ingredients together. Add to fruit mixture alternately with milk, beating well after each addition. Turn into a greased enamelled bundt pan, place into a 300 degree F. oven and bake for 3 hours. Place a large pan of hot water alongside the bundt pan of pudding in the oven for the 3 hour baking period. This will create the necessary moisture required to keep top of pudding moist. Serve with Butter Sauce. Keeps well. Serves 10-12.

Butter Sauce:

4 tbsp. butter
1 cup icing sugar
1/8 tsp. salt
1 tbsp. thick cream
1 tsp. vanilla, brandy or rum

Cream butter thoroughly, add sugar gradually and cream together until fluffy. Add cream and vanilla, beating well, about 3 minutes. Makes 3/4 cup.

HOME-MADE VANILLA ICE-CREAM

6 cups 18 per cent cream
1 cup sugar
1 tbsp. vanilla extract

Stir ingredients together for about 5 minutes until sugar dissolves. Pour into freezer can and churn according to directions. Put in refrigerator freezer 3 to 4 hours before serving. This recipe can be varied by adding 2 eggs, in which case you may want to use 2 cups of milk to replace 2 cups of the more expensive cream. The milk can be scalded. This helps dissolve the sugar, but also the mixture must be chilled before churning.

HOW TO FREEZE ANY ICE CREAM RECIPE

10 pounds of ice will be required to surround the inner freezer of the churn. A combination of salt and ice provides the freezing action, while the center blade inside the freezer can keep the ice cream mixture creamy and prevents ice crystals from forming. As you pack the ice into the bucket, add about two inches of ice and then sprinkle three tablespoons of salt over it — do this in layers until the bucket is filled. Do not use too much salt as this causes the outside layer of ice cream to freeze too fast and the churn to get stuck. Should this happen, open the freezer can, scrape down the ice cream mixture, stir it, and start again. Too little salt slows the freezing process.

There are two basic ways to make ice cream; uncooked, using cream and sugar; and cooked, which begins with the custard. The second produces a creamier, smoother ice cream, but it takes longer because the cooked custard has to cool and then be chilled before churning. Naturally, the heavier the cream used, the richer the ice cream. You can also substitute one cup of buttermilk for a cup of milk or cream. It is especially good in vanilla or banana ice cream.

OLD FASHIONED TAPIOCA PUDDING

4 tbsp. tapioca
4 cups milk
4 egg yolks
$^1/_2$ cup whipping cream
1 tbsp. sugar
1 tsp. vanilla

Soak the tapioca in water overnight. Heat milk to lukwarm, add soaked tapioca. Mix sugar and yolks together, add vanilla and stir into the tapioca mixture. Pour into a glass baking dish and bake for 1 hour at 325 degrees F. Cool. Frost with whipping cream which has been sweetened with 2 tsp. of sugar.

CHOCOLATE ICE CREAM

2 cups milk
4 cups 32 per cent cream (whipping cream)
6 egg yolks
1 cup sugar
4 oz. grated unsweetened chocolate
$^1/_4$ cup powdered cocoa
$^1/_2$ tsp. cinnamon

Mix powdered cocoa with 1 cup sugar in a large saucepan. Add egg yolks and beat well. Stir in milk and cream. Place over medium-low heat until slightly thickened, stirring constantly. Do not let this boil. Stir in remaining ingredients until smooth and chill immediately. Churn the mixture and freeze.

100

BANANA ICE CREAM

4 cups 32 per cent cream (whipping cream)
1 cup buttermilk
6 egg yolks
1 cup sugar
5 bananas, cut into pieces
1 tbsp. vanilla extract
1 tbsp. lemon juice

In a large saucepan make the custard with 2 cups of the cream, well-beaten egg yolks, buttermilk and $1/2$ cup of the sugar. Place over medium heat until smooth and slightly thickened. Do not let mixture boil. Blend bananas 30 seconds at high speed with the remaining sugar and cream. Blend in vanilla and lemon juice. Fold into the custard mixture and chill immediately. Churn and freeze.

PECAN PIE

6 tbsp. butter
$1/2$ cup granulated sugar
$1/2$ cup brown sugar
3 eggs
$1/2$ tsp. salt
$2/3$ cup corn syrup
$1/2$ cup maple syrup
1 tsp. vanilla
2 tsp. instant coffee
$1/2$ cup chopped walnuts
$3/4$ cup whole pecans
1 10-inch unbaked pie shell

Cream butter and sugars together; add eggs, one at a time and beat until light and fluffy. Add remaining ingredients, blending thoroughly. Pour mixture into the unbaked pie shell. Bake in a 400 degree F. oven for 20 minutes. Reduce heat to 325 degrees F. and bake for another 40 to 45 minutes, until the filling is set when tested with a knife. Serve with whipped cream.

Mom's Helpers

For a professional glaze on an open fruit pie or tart, try this: melt one cup of apple or currant jelly over a very low heat, stirring constantly. Cool the jelly a little, then spoon it over the cooled pie or tart. An apple jelly glaze looks best over apple, peach, banana or any other light-colored fruit. The currant jelly glaze complements strawberry, raspberry, plum or any other red fruit or berry.

CARROT PUDDING

  1 cup raw carrots, grated
  1 cup raw potato, grated
$^1/_2$ cup butter (if desired, $^3/_4$ cup chopped suet may be used instead of butter for a richer pudding)
  1 cup white sugar
$^3/_4$ cup seedless raisins
$^1/_2$ cup currants
$^1/_2$ cup candied mixed fruit
$^1/_2$ cup candied cherries, halved
  1 cup flour
$^1/_2$ tsp. cloves
$^1/_2$ tsp. nutmeg
$^1/_2$ tsp. cinnamon
  1 tsp. soda

Measure grated carrot and potato into a small bowl. Set aside. Cream butter well, gradually adding sugar. Add grated carrots and potatoes to butter mixture. Mix fruit together and dust it with $^1/_4$ cup flour. Add to butter mixture. Mix lightly. Mix remaining flour, spices, and soda together and add to butter mixture. Mix gently. Pour into a 2-quart buttered bowl. Cover with foil and tie it down with a string. Steam pudding for $4^1/_2$ hours.

LIGHT RUSSIAN DESSERT

  1 cup sugar
  1 envelope unflavoured gelatin
  4 eggs, separated
$^1/_2$ cup water
$^1/_8$ tsp. salt
  7 tbsp. vodka
  3 tbsp. coffee liqueur

Combine gelatin, $^1/_2$ cup sugar and salt. Mix well. Blend egg yolks, water, vodka and liqueur. Stir into gelatin mixture. Cover over medium heat until mixture comes to a boil. Remove from heat, chill until mixture is partially set. Beat egg whites until peaks form, then beat in $^1/_2$ cup of sugar into stiff peaks. Gently fold gelatin mixture into meringue and spoon into dessert glasses. Chill. Garnish with nutmeg, chocolate bits, and maraschino cherries. Serves 8.

Mom's Helpers

To get the maximum juice from a lemon, lime, or an orange, roll it on the counter, pressing down on it as you do to soften the fruit before you cut it.

DAIQUIRI DESSERT

1 cup sugar
1 envelope unflavoured gelatin
$1/8$ tsp. salt
4 eggs, separated
$1/2$ cup water
5 tbsp. white rum
2 tbsp. lime juice
2 tbsp. lemon juice

Combine gelatin, $1/2$ cup sugar and salt. Mix well. Blend egg yolks, water, rum, lime juice and lemon juice. Stir into gelatin mixture. Cook over medium heat until mixture boils. Remove from heat and chill until partially set. Beat egg whites until peaks form. Beat in $1/2$ cup of sugar until whites are stiff. Fold gelatin mixture into meringue and spoon into serving glasses. Chill. Serves 8.

LEMON CREAM SHERBET

2 cups milk
1 cup sugar
1 tbsp. finely grated lemon rind
$1/2$ cup lemon juice
2 egg whites
1 cup heavy cream, well chilled

Combine milk, $3/4$ cup sugar and lemon rind in a bowl. Stir in lemon juice slowly. Transfer mixture to an 8-cup freezer tray or shallow baking pan. Freeze about $1^1/4$ hours or until firm. Beat egg whites into soft peaks. Gradually add remaining $1/4$ cup sugar, beating all the time. Beat until whites form stiff peaks. Place in refrigerator. Wash the beater and rinse with cold water. Place 1 cup cream in a chilled bowl and whip until it holds shape. Do not overbeat. Break frozen lemon mixture into small pieces and turn into a large bowl. Beat until mixture fluffy and smooth. Fold in egg whites and whipped cream. Return mixture to 8 cup freezer tray or pan. Freeze for about $1^1/2$ hours or until sherbet is firm. The flavour mellows after the sherbet has been in the freezer for 2 or 3 days. Makes about 8 cups.

PINK CHERRY CREAM PIE

1 3-oz. pkg. flavoured gelatin
$1^1/2$ cups hot water
$1/2$ cup cherry preserve
1 cup heavy cream, whipped

Dissolve gelatin in hot water. When partially set, beat over ice water until fluffy. Fold in preserves and whipped cream. Chill until mixture is thick enough to mound. Pour into a baked pie shell. Chill for at least 1 hour before serving.

VANILLA ICE CREAM — CUSTARD BASE

6 egg yolks
1 cup sugar
2 cups milk
3 cups 32 per cent cream (whipping cream)
1 tbsp. vanilla extract

In a heavy saucepan whisk yolks and sugar together, then add milk in a stream. Stir over medium-low heat until smooth and slightly thickened, but do not let boil. Stir in cream and vanilla, let cool and then chill. Pour into a freezer can and churn. Store in the refrigerator freezer. Makes about 3 pints.

CREAM PUFFS

$^1/_4$ cup butter
$^1/_2$ cup boiling water
$^1/_2$ cup sifted all-purpose flour
$^1/_4$ tsp. salt
2 eggs, unbeaten

Add butter to boiling water in a saucepan, and heat until butter melts. Add flour and salt all at once, stirring vigorously. Cook until mixture leaves the sides of the pan. Remove from heat. Cool for 1 minute. Add eggs, unbeaten one at a time, beating with a spoon after each addition until smooth. Drop by tablespoon 2 inches apart on a greased sheet, shaping into mounds. Bake in a hot 450 degree F. oven for 10 minutes, then 400 degrees F. for another 25 minutes. Cool. Fill with whipped, sweetened cream.

SOUR CREAM PRUNE PIE

Pastry for a 9-inch pie crust
3 eggs
$1^1/_2$ cups finely chopped pitted prunes (not cooked)
$^1/_2$ cup sugar
$1^1/_2$ cups thick sour cream
$^1/_2$ cup chopped walnuts
1 tbsp. lemon juice
$^1/_4$ tsp. salt
$^1/_4$ tsp. ground cardamom or $^1/_4$ tsp. mace with $^1/_2$ tsp. nutmeg

Beat eggs. Stir in all remaining ingredients. Blend well. Pour into unbaked pie shell. Bake 10 minutes at 450 degrees F. then turn down heat to 350 degrees F. and continue baking for 30 minutes or until filling is set. Cool.

FRUIT OF THE VINE DESSERT

      1 lb. green seedless grapes
      2 (14-oz.) cans apricot halves
      2 (14-oz.) cans Bing cherries
    $^1/_2$ small lemon
  $1^1/_2$ cups granulated sugar
      1 cup light rum
    $^1/_2$ cup cognac or brandy

Remove grapes from stems and wash well. Drain apricots well. Drain canned cherries and pat dry with paper towels. Slice unpeeled lemon into rounds. Arrange fruit in jars, placing cherries on the bottom and lemon slices around the outside. Combine sugar, rum, and brandy in a bowl. Stir until sugar is almost dissolved. Pour over fruit mixture but do not mix. Cover and leave at room temperature in a dark place for 3 days, then refrigerate. Serves 8.

MARSHMALLOW TREATS

    $^1/_4$ cup butter
      4 cups marshmallows
    $^1/_2$ tsp. vanilla
      5 cups rice krispies

Combine butter and marshmallows in a heavy saucepan. Place over low heat, stir until marshamallows are melted. Stir in vanilla. Pour over rice krispies and mix well. Pour mixture into a 13 × 9 inch greased pan. Pat down. Sprinkle with colored coconut. Chill for 2 hours. Cut in desired sized squares and serve.

CHERRY TREATS

    $^1/_2$ cup butter
  $1^1/_3$ cups coconut
  $1^1/_2$ cups icing sugar
  $1^1/_2$ tsp. almond flavouring
      Maraschino cherries

Mix butter, coconut, icing sugar and flavouring together well. Pinch off about the size of a walnut, flatten out, place a maraschino cherry on it, and work with it to cover the cherry. Roll in crushed graham wafer. Chill for at least 2 hours and serve. Yields approx. 2 dozen covered cherry treats.

NO-FAIL PIE CRUST

    6 cups flour
    2 cups lard
    3 tsp. salt
 $^1/_2$ tsp. baking powder
    4 tbsp. brown sugar
    1 egg
    1 tbsp. vinegar
       cold water

Combine flour, salt, baking powder and brown sugar. Cut in the lard with a pastry cutter. Beat egg, add vinegar and water to fill 1 cup measure. Add $^1/_2$ the liquid mixture gradually to the flour mixture and toss with a fork. Dribble the remaining liquid mixture to moisten the dough so that it holds together when pressed between the finger tips. The exact amount of water needed in any given recipe depends on the temperature of the water, the temperature of the flour, the dryness of the flour, the temperature of the room, and the humidity of the atmosphere. Store in refrigerator for use. Will hold well without toughening.

PUMPKIN PIE

 $1^3/_4$ cups home-cooked or canned pumpkin
  $^3/_4$ cup brown sugar, firmly packed
  $^3/_4$ tsp. cinnamon
  $^1/_2$ tsp. ginger
  $^1/_2$ tsp. nutmeg
    1 cup light cream
  $^1/_2$ cup milk
    2 eggs, well-beaten

To make home-cooked pumpkin: Wash the outside of the pumpkin well, cut it in half and scoop out the seeds. Cut pumpkin into large pieces with the shell on, and place into a large heavy pot. Add 1 cup water, cover with lid, and cook for about ten minutes or until very tender. Remove from heat, drain, and cool. When pumpkin is cooled, you can easily scoop out the pulp from its shell and mash it with a potato masher or put it through a blender or food processor. Extra pumpkin can be frozen for future use.

To make filling: Drain off pumpkin liquid or place over low heat 10 minutes stirring often to dry out slightly. Heat oven to 450 degrees F. Combine sugar with next 4 ingredients. Stir into the very well beaten eggs. Place pie shell on oven rack when pouring in the filling. Bake at 450 degrees F. for 15 minutes; reduce heat to 300 degrees F. and bake 45 minutes or until a knife inserted half way into the center comes out clean. Cool on rack. Serve with whipped cream.

CREAMY RAISIN PIE

1 egg
1/2 cup sugar
1 1/2 cups raisins, washed
1/2 cup sour cream
1/4 tsp. cinnamon
Pinch of salt
1 tbsp. lemon juice
Pastry for two-crust pie

Beat egg with sugar until very light. Add raisins, cream, cinnamon, salt and lemon juice. Pour into the pie shell, cover the filling with a top shell, then make slits in the top shell with a sharp knife for air to escape as the pie is baking. Brush the top shell with a mixture of milk and egg beaten together to get a nice golden brown crust. Bake for 10 minutes at 450 degrees F., then lower temperature to 300 degrees F. and bake for 35-40 minutes, or until juice bubbles appear on the surface of the crust.

LAZY DAISY CAKE AND TOPPING

2 eggs
1 cup white sugar
1 cup flour
1/2 tsp. salt
1 tsp. baking powder
1 tsp. vanilla
1/2 cup milk
1 tbsp. butter

Beat eggs until light. Gradually add sugar. Sift together flour, salt, and baking powder. Add to egg mixture, blending well. Add vanilla. Heat up 1/2 cup milk with 1 tbsp. butter and add to egg mixture. Beat vigorously for 1 minute. Pour into a 9-inch square greased and floured pan and bake at 375 degrees F. for 30-35 minutes. Cover with the following topping immediately.

TOPPING

In a saucepan heat 5 tbsp. brown sugar, 3 tbsp. butter, 2 tbsp. whole milk and 1/2 cup coconut, stirring constantly. Cover cake as soon as it is baked and return to oven for a few minutes until the top bubbles. Remove from oven and cool in the pan.

Mom's Helpers

Add sugar to a tart or pie dough. Just one spoonful of sugar makes the crust bake to a beautiful golden brown.

MAPLE-PECAN ICE CREAM

2 cups 32 per cent cream (whipping cream)
2 cups maple syrup
3 cups milk
3 eggs, well beaten
1 1/2 cups chopped pecans
1/3 tsp. maple flavouring, if desired

In a large saucepan combine the cream and syrup and cook over medium heat, stirring until well blended. Add milk and eggs and continue to cook, stirring constantly, until slightly thickened and smooth, but do not let boil. Let cool. Stir in flavouring and let thoroughly chill. Stir in pecans into chilled mixture. Churn and freeze. Makes about 3 pints.

RUM RAISIN ICE CREAM

1 1/2 cup raisins
1 cup light or dark rum
6 egg yolks
1 cup sugar
1 cup buttermilk
2 cups 32 per cent cream (whipping cream)
2 cups whole milk
1 tbsp. vanilla

In a small saucepan combine raisins and rum. Bring to boil, reduce heat and simmer 5 minutes. Remove from heat and let raisins steep for one hour. Whisk together egg yolks and sugar. In a saucepan, bring next 3 ingredients to a simmer, then add to yolk mixture while stirring. Return egg-milk mixture to saucepan and stir over low heat until slightly thickened and smooth. Do not let boil. Stir in vanilla and chill immediately. Churn the custard mixture. Pour into the inner freezer can and churn. After the centre blade has been removed from the freezer can, drain raisins and stir them into the mixture. Freeze.

STRAWBERRY ICE CREAM

2 cups strawberries, slightly crushed
1/4 cup cherry brandy liqueur
1/4 cup orange liqueur
1 1/2 cups sugar
6 cups 32 per cent cream (whipping cream)

Combine strawberries, liqueurs and 1/2 cup of the sugar and let stand for 1 hour, then blend at high speed for 30 seconds. Mix cream and remaining sugar together until sugar dissolves. Fold in strawberry mixture. Churn and freeze.

MIX-IN-THE-PAN-BROWNIES

1/2 cup butter or shortening
2 squares unsweetened chocolate (2 oz.)
1 cup sugar
2 eggs
1 tsp. vanilla
1 cup all-purpose flour
1/2 tsp. baking powder
1/4 tsp. salt
1/2 cup chopped walnuts

Melt butter or shortening and chocolate in a 9-inch square cake pan at 350 degrees F. oven. Stir in sugar. Cool 5 minutes. Add eggs and vanilla, beat with fork until well blended. Sift flour, baking powder and salt into this mixture and mix well. Add nuts. Spread evenly in this pan and bake at 350 degrees F. for 30 minutes, until cake tester inserted into the center comes out clean. Cool on rack. Makes 2 dozen brownies.

CHILLED CHOCOLATE SOUFFLE

4 oz. semi-sweet baking chocolate
2 cups milk
1/3 cup water
2 tbsp. unflavoured gelatin
1/2 cup cold water
4 eggs, separated
1/2 cup sifted icing sugar
3 tsp. vanilla
2 cups whipping cream
Icing sugar
1 cup whipping cream
2 tbsp. icing sugar
1/4 tsp. cinnamon

Place chocolate in top of double boiler. Add milk and water and heat gently until chocolate is melted. Stir constantly. Soak gelatin in cold water for 5 minutes. Beat egg yolks in a small bowl until thick — about 5 minutes on high speed of mixer. Beat in 1/2 cup icing sugar. Add hot chocolate and stir to blend. Pour back into the top of the double boiler and simmer about 5 minutes. Stir constantly. Add gelatin and stir to dissolve. Remove mixture from heat and set in ice water to chill until it begins to mound when dropped from a spoon. Stir in vanilla. Beat egg whites until stiff. Beat 2 cups whipping cream until stiff. Fold cream into chilled chocolate mixture. Fold egg whites into chocolate mixture. Pour into a 2-quart souffle dish. Chill until firm — about 2 hours. Sift icing sugar thickly over the top. Whip remaining 1 cup cream with 2 tbsp. icing sugar and cinnamon just until it begins to thicken. Serve separately to pour over souffle.

MAPLE BUTTER TARTS

$^1/_2$ cup brown sugar
$1^1/_2$ cups maple syrup
 1 cup raisins
$^1/_4$ tsp. salt
 1 tbsp. butter
 2 beaten eggs
 1 tsp. vanilla
$^1/_2$ cup chopped walnuts or pecans
    Pastry for 18 medium sized tarts

Beat eggs well. Melt the butter and add to the beaten eggs. Stir in sugar, maple syrup, salt, and vanilla. Add raisins and nuts then spoon into unbaked tart shells $^2/_3$ full. Bake at 450 degrees F. for 8 minutes, then reduce heat to 350 degrees F. until pastry is golden and tarts are bubbly.

HOLIDAY CARROT PUDDING

$^1/_2$ cup ground suet
$^1/_3$ cup brown sugar
$^2/_3$ cup corn syrup
 1 egg
    Juice of 1 lemon
 2 tbsp. milk
 1 cup raisins
 1 cup currants
 1 cup grated raw potato
 1 cup grated raw carrot
$^1/_2$ cup flour
$^3/_4$ tsp. baking soda
$^1/_2$ tsp. salt
$^1/_2$ tsp. cloves
$^1/_2$ tsp. nutmeg
$^1/_2$ tsp. cinnamon
 1 cup fresh bread crumbs (3 slices of bread)

In a large mixing bowl, blend suet, sugar, corn syrup and egg. Add lemon juice and milk, blending thoroughly. Add raisins, currants, raw potato and carrot and stir well. Sift flour, baking soda, salt, cloves, nutmeg, and cinnamon over the mixture. Add crumbs and mix well. Turn into a well greased 5-cup mold ($^2/_3$ full to allow for expansion), cover with foil and steam for 3 hours.

Mom's Helpers

To tint coconut, place $1^1/_3$ cups flaked coconut in a jar. Add a few drops of food coloring. Screw on lid and shake until the coconut is colored.

LARGE PARTY CHEESECAKE

  1 cup all-purpose flour
  2 cups sugar
2^1/$_2$ tsp. grated lemon rind
 ^{1}/$_2$ cup cold butter
  1 egg yolk, lightly beaten
 ^{1}/$_2$ tsp. vanilla
  3 tbsp. flour
 ^{1}/$_4$ tsp. salt
  5 (8 oz.) pkgs. cream cheese (2^1/$_2$ lbs.) at room temperature
  1 cup whole eggs (5 to 6, depending on size)
  2 egg yolks
 ^{1}/$_4$ cup heavy cream

Combine 1 cup sifted flour, ^{1}/$_4$ cup sugar and 1^1/$_2$ tsp. lemon rind in a large bowl. Cut butter finely into the mixture. Add lightly beaten egg yolk and ^{1}/$_4$ tsp. vanilla, blend with a large fork. Use hands to shape dough into a ball. Divide into 3 equal portions. Evenly press 1 portion of dough over the bottom of a 9-inch springform pan (sides removed). Bake in a preheated oven, 400 degrees F. for about 8 minutes, until golden brown. Transfer to wire rack and allow to cool completely. Lightly butter sides of the pan and attach to cooled bottom. Evenly press remaining 2 portions of dough over the sides to a height of 2 inches.

Mix together remaining 1^3/$_4$ cups sugar, 3 tbsp. flour and salt. Beat cream cheese until it is fluffy; beat in remaining ^{1}/$_4$ tsp. vanilla and 1 tsp. lemon rind. Gradually add sugar mixture beating all the time. Add whole eggs and egg yolks, one at a time, beating well after each addition. Stir in cream; pour into prepared pan. Bake in preheated, very hot oven, 500 degrees F. for 5 minutes. Reduce oven temp. to 200 degrees F. and bake for 1 hour longer. Carefully transfer cheesecake to wire cake rack and allow to cool completely. When cake is cold, remove sides of pan. Cover and store cheesecake in a refrigerator. Served chilled, either plain or topped with Strawberry Glaze. Serves 12.

Strawberry Glaze:

Place 1 heaping cup of strawberries into a heavy saucepan. Crush berries with a wooden spoon. Add ^{1}/$_2$ cup sugar, 1 tbsp. corn starch and 1 tbsp. lemon juice. Mix well. Cook over low heat, stirring constantly, until mixture is thick and clear. Strain through a sieve and set aside to cool. Wash and hull 1^1/$_2$ cups strawberries which may be cut in half lengthwise. Arrange halves berries on top of the cheesecake, then spoon cooled glaze over them.

Mom's Helpers
To remove coconut meat from its shell most easily, heat the coconut in the hot oven a few minutes (until quite warm to the touch) before breaking the shell.

CREPES

   $3/4$ cup all-purpose flour
   1 tsp. baking powder
   $1/2$ tsp. salt
   2 tbsp. sugar
   2 eggs, well beaten
   $3/4$ cup milk
   $1/3$ cup water
   $1/2$ tsp. vanilla
   $1^1/2$ cups strawberry jam

Combine flour, baking powder, salt, and sugar. Add eggs, milk, water, and vanilla; mix until smooth. Cover and refrigerate for at least 2 hours. Heat a lightly greased 5-inch crepe pan or frying pan over medium heat. Pour about 1 tbsp. batter into the middle of the pan. Immediately tilt the pan in all directions to spread a thin film of batter over the entire surface of the pan. Cook until lightly browned, flip over and brown the other side lightly. Remove from pan. Roll up. Keep the crepes warm until all are cooked by placing them in a covered baking dish in the oven at 200 degrees F. Heat jam over medium heat. Spoon jam over warm crepes. Garnish with whipped cream and sliced almonds. Makes 14 to 16 crepes.

Note: Crepes may be prepared in advance for future use and frozen if they are stacked flat between layers of waxed paper. To use, thaw at room temperature. Roll up, place in a covered baking dish and re-heat at 200 degrees F.

TRADITIONAL STRAWBERRY SHORTCAKE

   2 cups all-purpose flour
   2 tbsp. sugar
   1 tbsp. baking powder
   $1/2$ tsp. salt
   $1/2$ cup butter
   $1/2$ to $3/4$ cup cream
   4 cups sliced strawberries, sweetened to taste
   1 cup whipping cream
   2 tbsp. orange juice or orange liqueur
   1 tbsp. sugar
   $1/2$ tsp. grated orange peel
   $1/8$ tsp. nutmeg

Stir together flour, sugar, baking powder and salt. Cut in $1/2$ cup butter until mixture resembles coarse crumbs. Blend in enough cream to make a soft dough. Turn onto lightly floured surface and knead gently for 30 seconds. Roll out $1/2$ inch thick. Cut out biscuits with floured 2-inch biscuit cutter; place on ungreased baking sheet. Bake at 450 degrees F. for 10 to 12 minutes or until lightly browned. Whip cream until soft peaks form, then gently whip in remaining ingredients. Split warm biscuits; butter each half. Spoon sweetened strawberries on the half then place other half on top with more strawberries. Top with whipped cream mixture. Makes approx. 12 biscuits.

NO-COOK STRAWBERRY JAM

4 cups fully ripe strawberries (approx. 1³/₄ cup crushed)
4 cups sugar
2 tbsp. lemon juice
6 tbsp. liquid fruit pectin

Wash, stem, and thoroughly crush strawberries and measure 1³/₄ cups into a large bowl. Mix sugar well into the crushed fruit and let stand 10 minutes. Add lemon juice and liquid fruit pectin to mixture. Stir for 3 minutes, until all sugar appears to have dissolved. Ladle quickly into jars and cover at once with tight lids. Let stand at room temperature until set (may take up to 24 hours), then store in the freezer. As a variation, add 1 tbsp grated orange rind to the strawberries and sugar mixture.

UNBAKED LIGHT CHEESECAKE

Crumb Crust:

2 cups graham wafer crumbs
2 tsp. cinnamon
6 tbsp. melted butter

Filling:

8 oz. plain cream cheese
¹/₂ cup sugar
¹/₈ tsp. salt
¹/₄ cup milk
1 tsp. lemon juice
1 tsp. vanilla
2 cups whipped cream

For crust, combine all ingredients in bowl and blend well. Press crumb mixture onto bottom and sides of a 9-inch pie plate. Bake at 400 degrees. F. for about 10 minutes. Cool completely. For filling, place cream cheese into large bowl, and with electric mixer, beat until smooth and light. Reduce speed and add sugar gradually, beating constantly. Add salt, milk, lemon juice and vanilla, continuing to beat until creamy. Fold whipped cream into mixture gently. Pile and swirl into baked shell and refrigerate for at least three hours. Top each serving with any fresh or canned fruit.

Mom's Helpers
Fruit jellies may be preserved from moldiness by covering the surface ¹/₄ inch with finely pulverized sugar. Thus protected, they will keep for years.

THE
LITTLE
"EXTRAS"

BEEF-SPAGHETTI SAUCE

2 tbsp. cooking oil
1 lb. ground beef
1 large sliced onion
2 cups meatless spaghetti sauce
2 cloves minced garlic
1 (6-oz.) can tomato paste
$^1/_2$ cup dry red table wine
1 cup water
1 bay leaf
1 tsp. oregano
6 peppercorns
$^1/_2$ tsp. salt

Heat oil in a large heavy saucepan. Add beef, onion, and garlic. Cook over medium-high heat stirring until the beef is well browned. Add remaining ingredients, turn down the heat, cover tightly and gently simmer 3 to 4 hours. If sauce becomes too thick, thin with red wine or water. Serves 4.

BROCCOLI WITH SOUR CREAM

1 lb. cooked broccoli
1 cup sour cream
2 tbsp. liquid honey
2 tbsp. cider vinegar
$^1/_2$ tsp. mustard
$^1/_4$ tsp. salt

Combine sour cream, honey, vinegar, mustard, and salt in a saucepan. Heat gently. Serve over hot broccoli. This is a sweet-sour sauce which combines nicely with broccoli.

CHEDDAR CHEESE FONDUE

2 tbsp. butter
2 tbsp. flour
1 tsp. Worcestershire sauce
$^1/_4$ tsp. dry mustard
1 bottle beer
3 cups old cheddar cheese, shredded
1 loaf medium rye bread, cut into cubes, crust on

Melt butter in a saucepan and blend in the flour. Stir in the Worcestershire sauce and mustard. Slowly add in the beer, stirring constantly until the mixture comes to a boil. Lower heat and add in cheese, stirring until cheese is melted. Remove from heat, pour into a fondue dish and place over a low burner. Use long handled forks on bread cubes to dip into the fondue. (If preferred, French bread may be substituted for medium rye).

116

CHEESE SPREAD PIQUANT

$1/4$ cup Worcestershire sauce
  2 tbsp. dry mustard
$1/2$ tsp. garlic powder
$1/4$ tsp. tabasco sauce
  8 oz. cream cheese
$1/4$ cup butter
$1^1/2$ tbsp. sherry

Mix Worcestershire sauce, mustard, garlic powder, sherry and tabasco sauce. Put cream cheese and butter into a bowl and beat with an electric beater until creamy. Dribble in Worcestershire sauce mixture slowly until all ingredients are thoroughly mixed. Transfer to a bowl and chill before serving. Makes 1½ cups. Delicious with crackers or in thin sandwiches.

COCKTAIL CHEESE BALL

  1 (7-oz.) can canned pink salmon
  1 (8-oz.) pkg. cream cheese
  2 tsp. Worcestershire sauce
$1/8$ tsp. pepper
  1 cup finely chopped nuts

Drain salmon well and mash with a fork. Combine with the next three ingredients, mix well, and chill thoroughly. Form into small balls about $3/4$-inch in diameter and roll in finely chopped nuts. Place a cocktail pick in each ball. Chill and serve. Makes about 30 appetizers.

DIET DIP

  1 cup cottage cheese
  2 tbsp. milk or buttermilk
  1 tbsp. lemon juice
  1 can (7½ oz.) salmon
  2 tsp. lemon juice
  2 tbsp. chopped green onion
$1/2$ tsp. prepared horseradish

In a blender or food processor, combine cottage cheese, milk and 1 tbsp. lemon juice. Set aside. Drain and flake salmon. Sprinkle with 2 tsp. lemon juice. Set aside cottage cheese and salmon mixture for one hour, then mix together with remaining ingredients and chill well. If mixture separates, stir before using. Makes 1½ cups.

DIETER'S YOGURT TREAT

- 2 cups plain yogurt
- 5 tbsp. oatmeal
- $1/2$ cup mixed nuts, roasted
- $1/2$ cup raisins
- $1/2$ cup skim milk
- 2 apples, coarsely shredded

Mix all ingredients together, mixing in the apples last. At this point the mixture will seem thin, but the oatmeal will thicken it after fifteen minutes. Add sugar or honey to taste. For a fruit salad, add oranges, peaches, grapes, etc. For a non-diet variation, top this salad with whipped cream.

HOT CRANBERRY SAUCE

- $1^2/3$ cups whole-berry cranberry sauce
- $1/2$ cup port wine
- 2 tbsp. honey
- 1 tsp. lemon juice

Combine all ingredients in a small saucepan. Cook over low heat until blended and warm. Serve as sauce with chicken, turkey, duck, or pork. (Do not boil ingredients — simply heat to below boiling point).

HOT CURRY SPREAD

- 4 tbsp. butter
- 2 tbsp. heaped, dry powdered milk
- 1 tbsp. curry powder
- 1 tsp. dry yeast
- 1 tsp. sugar
- 2 tbsp. peanut butter
- $1/2$ lemon, grated rind and juice

Beat all ingredients together to a creamy paste, adding more sugar, curry, or lemon juice to taste. Use for sandwiches or with dry or buttered toast. Serve with a glass of tomato juice. Keeps very well.

Mom's Helpers

Parsley stems impart as much flavour as the leaves. Use the parsley stems, whole or minced, for taste, and save the parsley leaves for garnishing.

LOBSTER SANDWICH SPREAD

2 cups flaked cooked lobster
$^1/_3$ cup chopped stuffed olives
3 hard cooked eggs, chopped
1 tsp. capers (optional)
$^1/_3$ cup mayonnaise
2 tsp. minced chives
$^1/_2$ cup diced celery

Combine all ingredients and chill for 1 hour.

RAW VEGETABLE DIP

$1^1/_2$ cups mayonnaise
2 tsp. curry powder
1 tbsp. grated onion
$^1/_2$ tsp. dry mustard
$^1/_3$ cup milk

Blend these ingredients together well. Serve with chunks of broccoli, celery, cauliflower, carrots, small tomatoes, zucchini. Excellent accompaniment for a cheese fondue feast.

SAUERKRAUT SALAD

$^1/_3$ cup vinegar
$^1/_3$ cup oil
1 cup sugar

Boil, stirring constantly, until sugar dissolves. Cool. Pour over:

3 cups drained sauerkraut
1 cup chopped onion
1 cup chopped green pepper
1 cup shredded carrots
1 cup diced celery

Let sit in the fridge overnight. (This will keep well in the fridge for several days).

Mom's Helpers

As a party snack or hors d'oeuvre, quiche may be prepared in mini-tart shells. Estimate 20 mini quiche for each 9-inch pie recipe.

SOUR CREAM AND CHEDDAR POTATOES

6 to 8 medium potatoes
1 cup sour cream
Salt and pepper to taste
¹/₂ cup chopped green onions or fresh chives
1 cup shredded cheddar cheese

Peel and boil potatoes in salted water. Drain and mash or whip with sufficient sour cream to give a light, creamy consistency. Add green onions, salt and white pepper to taste. Spoon into a buttered dish spreading evenly. Sprinkle the shredded cheddar cheese over top. Place into a 350 degree F. oven and bake until cheese is crusty and golden brown — 15 to 20 minutes. Serves 4 to 6.

SOUR CREAM DIP

¹/₂ cup mayonnaise
1 cup thick sour cream
¹/₃ cup milk
1¹/₂ tbsp. finely chopped green onion
1 tbsp. fresh dill, finely chopped
1 tbsp. fresh parsley, finely chopped
¹/₂ tsp. seasoned salt

Combine all ingredients and mix very well. Chill for several hours before serving. (The fresh dill and parsley may be substituted by dried dill and parsley).

SUNSHINE PARTY SPREAD

2 cups grated old cheddar cheese
¹/₂ cup soft butter
3 green chopped onions
3 to 4 tsp. rum
¹/₄ tsp. dry mustard

Blend ingredients together until smooth with an electric mixer or a food processor. Spoon into a serving dish, cover with foil and chill overnight. Serve with crackers.

Mom's Helpers
Parsley is easier to chop after it has been washed in hot water very briefly and then dried in a paper towel.

YORKSHIRE PUDDING

$^1/_2$ cup plain white flour
 1 egg
$^1/_2$ cup water
$^1/_2$ cup milk
 1 tsp. melted butter
$^1/_8$ tsp. salt
     Beef or pork roast drippings

Sift flour with salt in a large bowl. Hollow out center, drop in the egg and $^1/_2$ of the liquids. Mix from the center — egg and water first, then add remaining milk. Add melted butter. Beat very well, preferably with a beater, until smooth and shiny. Let stand for 10 minutes. Pour in 1 tsp. of roast drippings into each cup cake container (a tin of 8 cups). Pour mixture into tins, dividing equally. Place into a hot (450 degree F.) oven for 10 minutes. Lower temperature and continue baking for 10 to 15 minutes. Serve with beef roast. Top each pudding with $^1/_4$ cup gravy.

Mom's Helpers

For a colorful garnish that is simple to make, cut peeled lemons or oranges into $^1/_4$ inch thick slices, making sure to remove the white pith and seeds. Cut slices in half, then roll them in finely-minced parsley or paprika as desired.

BRANDY TREAT

1 can sweetened milk
12 oz. brandy
2 cups whipping cream
1 tbsp. cocoa
1/2 tsp. coconut or almond extract
3 eggs, beaten

Blend all ingredients in a blender. Refrigerate for at least 2 hours before serving. Serves 5-6.

HOT MULLED WINE

1/2 cup sugar
1 cup water
2 long cinnamon sticks (3-inch)
12 whole cloves
Dash of nutmeg
1 lemon
3 cups red or white dry wine

Combine sugar, water, and spices in saucepan. Peel lemon and drop whole peel into sugar mixture. Stir to dissolve sugar. Simmer 5 minutes. Remove from heat and let stand 30 minutes. Add wine and heat slowly to just under boiling point. Serve hot. Serves 6.

IRISH COFFEE

1 cup brewed coffee
1 1/2 oz. Irish whiskey
1 heaping tbsp. sweetened whipped cream
Sugar to taste
Nutmeg

Into each glass, pour 1 1/2 oz. Irish whiskey. Add hot coffee to one-inch from the top (pour coffee slowly over a spoon set into the glass to prevent breakage of glass). Sweeten to taste then top with whipped cream. Sprinkle nutmeg over the whipped cream and serve.

Mom's Helpers

Before making a flambe with any liqueur, brandy, or whiskey, be sure to heat it. It will not ignite unless it is hot.

ORANGE COOLER

 3 cups cold milk
 1 cup chilled orange juice
 4 eggs
 $^1/_3$ cup liquid honey
 2 cups ice cream
 1 cup vodka

Blend all ingredients in a blender until frothy. Pour into chilled glasses, sprinkle cinnamon on top and serve. Serves 6.

OLD FASHIONED EGG NOG

 6 eggs, separated
 $^1/_2$ cup sugar
 2 cups light cream
 1 cup whole milk
 10 oz. brandy or white rum
   Dash of salt
 $2^1/_2$ cups whipping cream
   Nutmeg

With electric beater beat egg yolks until fluffy and gradually beat in salt and sugar. Slowly beat in cream, milk, and brandy or rum. Fold in whipped cream and stiffly beaten egg whites. Chill for 3 hours. When ready to serve, sprinkle each drink with nutmeg. Serves 6 to 8.

ORANGE FIZZ

 4 cups chilled orange juice
 3 cups softened sherbet
 5 cups ginger ale, chilled
 $1^1/_2$ cups gin
   Orange slices for garnish

Combine orange juice and sherbet in punch bowl, using a wire whip. Slowly stir in ginger ale and gin. Mix well. Serve in punch cups, garnished with orange slices. Serves 10 to 12.

Mom's Helpers

When serving hot beverages in glasses, pour hot liquid into the glass over a spoon placed into the glass to prevent breakage.

SPICED APRICOT

 4 cups apricot nectar
 7 thin slices lemon
 2 cinnamon sticks
12 whole cloves
 6 whole allspice
$3/4$ cup apricot brandy or orange flavoured liqueur

Combine apricot nectar, lemon slices, and cinnamon sticks in 2-quart sauce-pan. Tie cloves and allspice in a cheesecloth. Add to nectar. Simmer gently — 15 minutes. Remove spice in cheesecloth bag. Just before serving, add apricot brandy or orange liqueur, pour into mugs, and garnish with a lemon slice dipped in sugar. Serves 4 to 6.

TANGY SLUSH

 7 cups boiling hot water
 3 tea bags
12 oz. frozen yellow lemonade
12 oz. frozen orange juice
26 oz. lemon gin or vodka

Steep the tea bags in 2 cups water for 5 minutes, then remove the tea bags. Add 5 remaining cups of boiling water, frozen lemonade and orange juice. Let dissolve. Add 26 oz. of gin or vodka. Stir. Pour into large wide mouth jar and place into the keep freeze for overnight. The mixture will freeze, forming a soft ice. To use, spoon into serving glass $3/4$ full, then add gingerale to fill glass. Garnish with an orange slice and serve.

COOL MILKSHAKE

 2 cups milk
$1/4$ cup maple syrup
 4 cups maple walnut ice cream

In a blender combine milk, syrup, and 1 cup ice cream. Blend until smooth and gradually add the remaining ice cream. Continue to blend until smooth. Serves 4.

Mom's Helpers

To keep water taps bright and shiny, put a few drops of lysol on a damp cloth, wipe taps, then rinse and dry.

HOT RUM PUNCH

    1 gallon apple cider
    1 cup dark rum
    1 cup brandy
    3 cinnamon sticks
$^1/_2$ tsp. whole mace
$^1/_2$ tsp. whole allspice

Combine ingredients in a large saucepan. Simmer gently over low heat for 30 minutes and serve hot. Serves 35.

MINT DELIGHT

    6 cups milk
    4 tbsp. sugar
 $1^1/_2$ tsp. peppermint extract
    5 to 6 drops green food coloring
       Pinch of salt
    1 pint vanilla ice cream
       Pineapple chunks

Add sugar, peppermint, food coloring and salt to cold milk, stirring to blend. Pour into cold glasses, top with vanilla ice cream and garnish with pineapple chunks. Serves 6.

ORANGE FROSTY

 $1^1/_2$ cups buttermilk
 $^1/_3$ cup undrained crushed pineapple
    2 tbsp. sugar
    3 large scoops orange sherbet

In a blender combine buttermilk, crushed pineapple, sugar and sherbet. Cover and blend at high speed until smooth. Serves 3.

Mom's Helpers
Happiness is a perfume you cannot pour on others without getting a few drops on yourself.